Rethinking
School Mathematics

Rethinking
School Mathematics

Andrew Noyes

Paul Chapman
Publishing

First published 2007

Paul Chapman Publishing
SAGE Publications Company
1 Oliver's Yard
55 City Road
London EC1Y 1SP

SAGE Publications Inc
2455 Teller Road
Thousand Oaks, California 91320

SAGE Publications India Pvt Ltd
B 1/I 1 Mohan Cooperative Industrial Area
Mathura Road, Post Bag 7, New Delhi 110 044
India

SAGE Publications Asia-Pacific Pte Ltd
33 Pekin Street #02-01
Far East Square
Singapore 048763

Library of Congress Control Number: 2006939576

British Library Cataloguing in Publication data

A catalogue record for this book is available
from the British Library

ISBN 978-1-4129-2102-2
ISBN 978-1-4129-2103-9 (pbk)

Typeset by C&M Digitals (P) Ltd., Chennai, India
Printed in Great Britain by Athenaeum Press, Gateshead, Tyne & Wear
Printed on paper from sustainable resources

CONTENTS

ACKNOWLEDGEMENTS

Many individuals have been influential in the writing of this book but particular mention needs to be made of my mathematics teacher education colleagues at the University of Nottingham: Peter Gates, Kieran Murphy, Stef Sullivan and Mark Simmons. They have been supportive throughout and willing to read parts of the manuscript at various stages of completion. That is not to say that they would agree with everything that is written herein, but their openness to considering the complexities of mathematics education is sustaining. Hilary Povey and Linda Haggarty are due special mention for their helpful comments on drafts of the manuscript. Many other mathematics educators and scholars have been influential in shaping the ideas of this volume, not least because I am aware of not being alone in thinking that there must be a better way to do mathematics education in schools. Some of these people I know well and others I know only through their writing. Nevertheless I am pleased to be part of what is a global debate about the purposes of school mathematics.

Secondly I want to thank the four beginning teachers who read the manuscript and were so positive in response: Katia, Anneke, Joe and James. I hope that you are able to make use of the ideas in the book and that you will keep questioning the *status quo* and, when necessary, go against the flow of tradition and current trend in pursuit of a more socially just, relevant and engaging mathematics education.

Finally, thanks to Helen Fairlie at Sage who saw something in this book proposal and who has been encouraging and patient throughout.

INTRODUCTION

This book explores some big questions concerning mathematics education – questions that I think every teacher of mathematics should consider from the outset of their career. These include:

- Why teach mathematics?
- Of what use is the mathematics curriculum to different groups of learners?
- Why are popular views of mathematics often so negative and what might teachers do in an attempt to challenge these?
- Where has mathematics education come from and where is it going? Who decides?
- How does/can mathematics contribute to general education; young people's personal, social, spiritual, moral and cultural development?

The issues with school mathematics education explored herein cannot be resolved once and for all. In our changing world, school mathematics, perhaps more than any other curriculum area, is subject to the competing perspectives and controlling influences of various groups in society. These perspectives are not only intellectual, but ideological, political and historical, and as you read this book you will be invited to reflect upon your own position in relation to these themes. If you are someone concerned about mathematics teaching and learning in schools, you probably have fairly strong beliefs about the subject and how best it should be taught and learnt; though you might not be fully aware of them. This book will help you to explore those beliefs and practices and enable you to recognize that your position is not neutral.

This is not an impersonal textbook but is intended to provoke a response in you; to make you think about the complex issues of teaching school mathematics. Provoking people can be a risky business but my aim is to make you think, to see the work of teaching mathematics as intellectual, political, cultural and social. Perhaps the book should therefore come with a health warning, namely, that I would not expect every reader to agree with every argument and position. Moreover the classroom activities and ideas in Part II might not interest you. Such difference is good as the world would be rather dull place if we all thought the same things and agreed on everything. Although this is one person's account of where we are now *at* and where mathematics teaching might *go,* you will find many references to literature that you can read in order to explore these ideas further.

When I moved from teaching secondary school mathematics into higher education, initially to work with those learning to become teachers of mathematics, I had some nagging concerns about the nature of what I had been doing as a teacher of mathematics and the impact that it had had upon learners. At that time I had not formulated those concerns into meaningful questions, let alone managed to answer them in a convincing way. On the whole I enjoyed my own schooldays and, being in the top groups for mathematics, had also enjoyed the privilege (and unfairness) of being taught by those considered to be the best teachers in the school. After an uninspiring undergraduate degree, I started to teach in a school with a rich tradition of curriculum innovation. One of the authors of the South Notts. Project (Bell, Rookey and Wigley, 1979) had been a previous head of department and an investigative, creative tradition had continued until the early 1990s when I joined the school. It was in that school and departmental culture that I learned to teach mathematics. I am indebted to my colleagues, and in particular to Sue Pope, my first head of department, who inspired me to keep thinking about innovative pedagogy, ethnomathematics (though I did not know it was that at the time), the value of collaborative learning, rich learning environments, and so on. Many children in that school learned their mathematics in all-ability groups, but this was not to last for long as the 1990s brought huge changes to the culture of UK schools. First the National Curriculum, then national Key Stage tests, Office for Standards in Education (Ofsted) inspections, school league tables and, by the time I left that school, Curriculum 2000 had happened – with disastrous effect for mathematics – and Key Skills (including Application of Number) had come ... and nearly gone. That department had in many ways been transformed by the new performance and audit culture of the education market.

I am not suggesting that this department was perfect by any means, but rather I want to signal that during those transition years, with all of the changes of staff and policy developments, something was lost. The way that mathematics was being experienced in school had shifted and the root cause of this was the so called 'standards' agenda. So it was that I began to understand the political nature of knowledge, including mathematical knowledge. I also came to realize that even the liberal mathematics learning culture that I had known was not explicitly addressing relationships between mathematics, society, culture and power; this will be a central theme of this book. So, for the last five years I have been trying to make sense of this, not as an interested observer standing apart from the transitional turbulence of curriculum change and policy experimentation, but as someone still in the mix, caught up in mathematics education at a crucial time in its development, albeit with a particular historical view. I cannot claim that this book is impartial, but then neither can any of us when it comes to understanding our beliefs and practices. However, in exploring possible alternatives and missing ingredients in current school mathematics lessons, I hope that you will be encouraged to understand more fully your own views on mathematics education and the implications that this might have for classroom teaching and learning, and for learners themselves. This reflective journeying will include you mapping out your own part of the terrain in which you have learned and are now teaching mathematics. You will recognize certain freedoms and constraints that you have and are now enjoying, and understanding these features is important in your ongoing development as a teacher of mathematics.

This book is written primarily for teachers of mathematics but also those who are concerned with the challenges of mathematics education. It is grounded in the context of English school mathematics education and explores popular, ongoing national antipathy to things mathematical. However, the issues considered might well be of interest to mathematics educators in other countries who share similar concerns about the social role of mathematics education.

Part I explores questions about the nature of school mathematics, with brief recourse to history, references to culture and an overview of the changing national policy context for school mathematics. International comparisons (for example, TIMSS, PISA) have resulted in 'reform' education policies in many countries, and so it is not only mathematics educators in England who are questioning the nature of teaching and learning mathematics. Since the late 1980s, a series of policies have sought to improve the teaching and learning of school mathematics. Academics, politicians and education commentators differ in their views on how successful these initiatives have been. Such political work is far from over, as during the writing of this book we will have moved from three- to two-tier General Certificate of Secondary Education (GCSE) system; new pathways through 14–19 mathematics will have been devised and published; students will be learning 'functional mathematics' alongside their traditional exam syllabuses. Moreover, we now have a National Centre for Excellence in the Teaching of Mathematics (with a budget of £15 million for its first three years!). Why then, with all of this effort and money expended on improving the quality of school mathematics education, do so many still love to hate mathematics?

The chapters in Part I will develop your broader understanding of mathematics education and provide some rationale for exploring alternative (but complementary) classroom activities. Part II extends the consideration of the purpose of school mathematics and its relevance for the twenty-first-century citizen by bringing together a collection of classroom approaches and resources that develop some of the themes from Part I. There are plenty of resources that support the development of high-quality teaching of mathematics. Numerous existing books offer plenty of food for thought and the Internet – combined with increasing interactive capability – allows you access to the best ideas (and the worst!) from across the world. However, this overwhelming volume of material can distract from asking the big questions about what we teach in mathematics classrooms, why and how we teach it, and what the outcomes are for the learner. So Part II will focus on ways of thinking about classroom mathematics that take account of social, cultural, political and historical contexts in which mathematics has developed and is now used. Of course these ideas are not new but, hopefully, you will find some of them brought together in a way that might be helpful when exploring alternatives to the current trends of mathematics teaching.

Although you will be encouraged to develop a broader view of mathematics learning in school you should not expect this to be an alternative textbook. Critically appraising, selecting and redesigning learning tasks should always be a fundamental aspect of teachers' work, so this book is not intended as a 'how to do', but rather a 'how to think' about the teaching and learning of mathematics. This is an important point but, in an age where mathematical *instruction* and rule-following takes precedence over *education* and exploratory learning, this is not always welcomed. For example, David, a beginning teacher said of his Postgraduate Certificate of Education (PGCE) course: 'I thought that we would learn to teach, or we would be taught to teach mathematics, whereas we're taught to think about teaching mathematics. And one of the problems that I can see with that, is that, basically, that I will teach things the way that I was taught.' I do not think that the first point made by David automatically leads to the second but the principle that he hints at is important, namely, that how you experienced mathematics has a strong influence over how you might teach it (Noyes, 2004b). What he means by 'being taught' is being instructed or trained, which is not what he got. Rather he was being educated to think for himself, to learn the craft of teaching which is intellectual, experimental, creative and always developing. Stuart, another beginning teacher who had struggled with his own mathematics education, described his experiences as follows:

> I don't blame myself only for struggling. I think it were the teaching. You worked from the SMP Y series, the yellow books. You basically walked in and sat down and 'right, get on with where you left off'. In my time at school I very rarely remember the maths teacher up at the board. I remember the maths teacher I had for my GCSEs, she were just sat at the front desk: all lesson, every lesson. 'If you've got any problems just come and sit next to me and see me'.

Stuart found the whole-class interactive components of teaching difficult to develop and although I do not want to suggest a direct causal relationship here it is worth you thinking about how your own learning story is influencing your teaching. One of my hopes for David, Stuart and for you as a reader of this book is that you might develop critical dispositions towards teaching. Brookfield (1987, cited in Scott, 2000: 3) described four dimensions of criticality as:

- identifying and challenging assumptions
- challenging the importance of context
- imagining and exploring alternatives
- developing reflective scepticism.

These four dimensions give a good idea of what you might expect to be engaged with through the remainder of this book. First, I hope to challenge your assumptions about the teaching and learning of mathematics and to get you involved in what Ulrich Beck (1994) terms 'self-confrontation'. That is not to say that you will necessarily change your position but, hopefully, you will be more aware of it and be able to justify your views. You will be thinking about the historical and political context of mathematics education and will be invited to imagine some alternatives. Finally, I hope that you develop that sense of reflective scepticism about the value and effectiveness of school mathematics. This should not mean a wholly negative view of what happens in classrooms, but rather a more realistic, critically informed view, which might inspire you to play a small part in *rethinking school mathematics*.

The many excellent resources concerned with the principles and practicalities of constructing high-quality mathematics learning experiences have been referred to above. A large part of mathematics education research has been concerned with understanding mathematical cognition and how teaching can be designed to improve learning. Given this wealth of knowledge, it is interesting that many young people do not have positive experiences of learning mathematics and I want to explore the possible reasons for this. Furthermore, I doubt whether (1) the application of current knowledge is sufficient to affect the kind of transformation in mathematics education that so many people are calling for, and (2) this is the right way to move. A change in direction, or shift in emphasis, is required. That is not to suggest that good teaching and learning (however one defines it) that exists already should be overlooked. On the contrary, as a community of mathematics educators we need to strive for increased quality of mathematics learning for all students in schools. However, the message of this book is that currently there are missing threads in school mathematics and these need to be woven into the fabric of existing quality teaching.

Indirectly, this is a book written for all those children who have not been served well by traditional mathematics teaching and curriculum; those who have found their mathematics education uninspiring and irrelevant. Whether or not it will serve to help any of these students remains to be seen. That is not to say that my vision for mathematics education is for one group over another, but rather there should be developments that will benefit all young people. One of the arguments you will be considering is that mathematics education in secondary schools should reflect the broader aims of *general education*. This was Hans Werner Heymann's (2003) argument regarding German mathematics education, which provoked considerable discussion about many of the same issues that you will be thinking about when reading this book. For his context he cautions that 'the path to instruction oriented more strongly toward general education cannot be enforced from external sources ... but can only consist of small steps involving many participants for whom these steps make good sense' (Heymann, 2003: 84). So this book is my attempt to mark a pathway to a more engaging, equitable, democratic mathematics education and to invite you to consider walking this way – if it makes 'good sense'.

When Nel Noddings (2004) briefly outlined a possible alternative direction for US mathematics curricula at the 2004 American Education Research Association's annual conference, she described her vision as 'an exercise of the imagination'. Hopefully, this book will exercise you in the same way. My aim is to get you thinking about some alternative directions for school mathematics education that might be better suited to the needs of all citizens, particularly those of the majority: school students who will not proceed to study advanced mathematics courses beyond their compulsory schooling. In so doing, this book will hopefully provoke discussion amongst teachers and other mathematics educators about the best way to steer a course towards a mathematics education fit for the young learners of the twenty-first century. And if you do feel provoked but do not agree with what I am arguing for, then I would encourage you to develop your own arguments and position on these matters.

Finally, some thoughts on how you might engage with the book. Parts I and II are quite different in their aims and style. You will be able to dip into the chapters of Part II or read them through as a whole. They contain ideas for classroom activities. However, they are not tasks that can be lifted straight into your own classrooms; rather they are starting points and processes that you might tailor to your own classroom contexts. The earlier chapters require a more traditional reading but do have a number of questions and reflection points that should help to get you thinking about the issues. I would recommend that you take some time to record something in response to these questions for it is all too easy to skip over them. This need not be in any particular form; diagrams, concept maps, lists would all be fine. You might have emotional responses to the questions or feel that you are not in a position to answer them. All this is fine but, in keeping with the critical focus that I am asking you to adopt, do try and make some sense of these various responses. Most people who read this book will be pre- or in-service teachers of mathematics, which means that the range of questions and tasks are aimed at teachers at quite different points in their careers. So use them as you see fit. Knowing that I never read a book like this when I was a teacher presents me with a certain challenge – to make you want to read on whilst at the same time not oversimplifying the issues. I congratulate you for having got this far!

I firmly believe that the work of teaching is deeply intellectual and so this book does try to engage you with some big ideas, research and theory. However, I hope that you will find what follows both intellectually stimulating and helpful for critical reflection upon, and the development of, both your teaching and students' learning of mathematics. I would be very happy for you to let me know whether or not I have managed to do this.

andrew.noyes@nottingham.ac.uk
November 2006

PART I

Before starting on this part of the book you should take some time to reflect on your own mathematical learning journey. The following questions might be helpful in doing this:

- What experiences of learning mathematics have you enjoyed/endured up to this point? How were you taught mathematics, both at school and beyond? Were these teaching styles effective for all learners? Why?
- What were your reasons for becoming a teacher of mathematics?
- What mathematics do you think should be a part of the curriculum (that is, what is important mathematics) and how do you think it would be best learnt/taught? What counts as good learning of mathematics and if you needed to evaluate this learning what would be a good measure?
- You might also like to consider what mathematics is (this is not an easy question to think about, let alone answer) and how it is used in society.
- How do you, your colleagues, and your students use mathematics in their daily lives? Does any of this relate to what they do in the classroom?

MATHEMATICS – THE SUBJECT
WE LOVE TO HATE

This chapter sets the scene for what follows in this book. Why and how does a general antipathy towards things mathematical get perpetuated in schools and society? What part does school mathematics play in the production and reproduction of such attitudes? We will also begin to question the various roles that mathematics has in the school curriculum and how these might be reconceptualized. Who is well served by school mathematics and how should the twenty-first-century citizen be educated mathematically? This is of course a political question and this chapter introduces the socio-political thread that weaves through the chapters. The important and complex questions introduced here will be explored in greater depth through the first part of the book.

'I HATE MATHEMATICS'

Some years ago I used to mark intermediate level General Certificate of Secondary Education (GCSE) papers for one of the UK examinations boards. There are few highlights to this mundane work, but a handful of papers stick in my memory, and one in particular raised an important question. When asked to complete a trigonometry question in this final school mathematics examination one candidate scrawled a frustrated 'I DON'T BLOODY KNOW' across the page, and on the next page an equally emphatic 'I HATE MATHEMATICS'. The sense of exasperation was clear, and I suspect that this candidate felt they were not doing too well! After my initial amusement the person behind the paper drifted into my thoughts and for a moment the examination paper belonged to a real person. Though probably prompted by anger, these comments reflect a deeper sense that this student has of the power of schooling, assessment and mathematics. The French sociologist, Pierre Bourdieu, described how, 'Often with a psychological brutality that nothing can attenuate, the school institution lays down its final judgements and its verdicts, from which there is no appeal, ranking all students in a unique hierarchy of all forms of excellence, nowadays dominated by a single discipline, mathematics' (Bourdieu, 1998: 28).

This particular student was experiencing the *psychological brutality* of *final judgement* and was not enjoying the process. Bourdieu described such boundaries as the GCSE C/D borderline as a 'magical threshold' whereby two students, separated by the narrowest of margins, can have their future educational and life opportunities differentiated in an instant. Such educational magic divides the 'profane' – grade D and below – from the 'sacred' – grades C and above (to use another sociologist, Emile Durkheim's terms). It might seem harsh to make this division between the sacred and profane but this issue has been at the heart of a long-running debate about the structure of GCSE mathematics. This separation of learners by the C/D threshold is one dimension of the power of mathematics as currently constructed in the curriculum.

Of all the school subjects, mathematics is most likely to hinder progression towards further and higher education and employment opportunities. With its arbitrarily maintained pass marks, GCSE mathematics grade C is the most sacred of examination results. But this is so for schools as well as for individual learners. In our performativity culture (Ball, 2003) where league table position is critical, and dependent upon C-grade attainment, the potency of such mathematical branding is all too apparent. Schools that have succeeded in raising the proportion of students with five or more higher grade passes at GCSE are now faced with the prospect of having to include GCSE mathematics and English as part of the new GCSE Diploma. This will impact certain types of schools more than others, particularly those in more challenging circumstances that have used double GCSEs and General National Vocational Qualifications (GNVQs) to bolster attainment.

SO WHAT COUNTS AS SUCCESS?

Returning to our beleaguered GCSE exam candidate, let us assume, for sake of argument, that this student achieved a grade C. Was that achievement a success? Or perhaps we might ask a different question: had this student's mathematics education been successful? Your response to this question depends upon your criteria for success, and these will vary for different teachers, pupils, schools and parents. At one level, obtaining that magical grade C is good news for the school's league table position. In addition, it probably confers the potential privileges of further and higher education access for the student. However, I would hazard a guess that this candidate will not be keen to continue studying mathematics and will probably be quite happy to see the back of the subject. So although 'successful' in one sense, this student is now another contributor to a culture that generally views mathematics negatively and probably has little interest in using it or understanding how the world is being 'formatted' (to use Ole Skovsmose's 1998 term) through the impact of mathematically rooted science and technology, economics and social science.

THE POLITICS OF KNOWLEDGE

Straightaway we have raised issues about the politics of knowledge, in particular mathematical knowledge, and how this is realized in the school curriculum, pedagogy and more widely in society. G.H. Hardy, the celebrated twentieth-century pure mathematician, famously pronounced that his mathematical work was of no practical use whatsoever. In recent years this has been shown to be far from the case and the abstract number theory of which he was so proud now underpins the security of our technologically networked society. However, it is also equally apparent that beliefs about the discipline of mathematics, particularly those held by influential academics, educators and politicians, have the power to shape the curriculum and societal attitudes more generally. The dominant view among these powerful groups is that mathematics, at the core of the political standards-raising agenda, is one of the keys to future economic prosperity. Indeed the Chancellor, Gordon Brown, has pronounced that science (and I include mathematics here) is the 'bedrock of our economy'. This is not only because of the need for science, technology, engineering and mathematics (STEM) graduates but also a demand for mathematically skilled workforce. So mathematics is at the core of the National Curriculum (NC) owing to its supposed economic and political value.

The mathematics NC claims that 'mathematics equips pupils with a uniquely powerful set of tools to understand and change the world' (p. 14). Along with many of my non-mathematician colleagues I would contest the uniqueness of mathematics to understand and change the world. Although the second part of this description is potentially a healthy goal for any curriculum, the use of the engineering metaphor of 'tools' is constraining. The curriculum needs to move beyond a predominantly utilitarian view of mathematical knowledge, and we will explore this in more depth in Chapter 3. Mathematics teachers should also remember that the changes inspired by mathematics have not all been for the good of humanity: I would not like to guess at how many mathematicians are employed in the design and manufacture of arms, for example.

Many scholars have highlighted how mathematics education functions in society to perpetuate inequality in ways that need critique and redress. This brings us back to the issue of power. The quote from the NC above refers to the equipping of students with a powerful set of tools, but perhaps it is as important for these learners to understand how mathematics is a powerful set of tools used, actively and passively, on them as citizens by various groups. This is the *formatting* power of mathematics.

MATHEMATICS CURRICULAR AIMS

If mathematical applications in society shape our lives in many complex and often hidden ways, then one of the aims of the mathematics curriculum should be to uncover, explain and empower learners to critique those *formatting* processes (Skovsmose, 1994). Such a broadening of the aim of mathematics education is far from straightforward and gets us to the nub of the issues explored in the following chapters, which is the nature and purpose of education, and what it means to be an educated citizen in the twenty-first century. Peter Gill concludes his analysis of the effectiveness of the mathematics NC like this:

> the current curriculum for mathematics fails to meet the claims made for it in mathematical terms and also fails to contribute to the overall ethos of the National Curriculum contained in the *Aims and Values*. Nothing less than a complete overhaul is necessary if it is to serve our pupils and the society they, and we, live in. (Gill, 2004: 115)

I agree with this view and will return to those aims and values in Chapter 5 and the second part of the book. But how might a complete overhaul of the curriculum happen and what would be the impact upon you and your students? This is a big question but, hopefully, one to which there are some possible initial lines of approach. We will get to those by the end of the book. Whilst things remain as they currently stand, many children will be failed by their mathematics education, not necessarily through the fault of any one teacher but because of the structure of school and the nature of the curriculum.

MATHEMATICAL TRAJECTORIES

One such learner is 10-year-old Stacey who, in her final year at primary school, confided to her video diary that she was compiling 'now mathematics, boring, boring, boring. Three things about mathematics, I hate it! I hate it! I hate it!' But just how common is this view of mathematics? Surveys of children moving from primary to secondary school suggest that the greatest cause of anxiety at the transition is mathematics (Galton et al., 2002). This is the case for all but high-attaining boys. What is not clear from that research is whether this says something about the impact of primary school mathematics, the reputation of secondary school mathematics and mathematics teachers or some complex amalgam of these two and other social effects. Stacey, a relatively 'low attainer', did not fare well with her mathematics in the transition to secondary school but her negative learner identity was already well established before the move. Following her comments above she explained:

> The thing that makes mathematics hard for me is that I don't think I'm really good at it ... erm ... I have to say this prufully, I mean trufully ... erm ... I know what everyone's thinking, that ... I'm the dumbest kid in the class ... and me and Sonya really need desperate help. I'm not saying that she's bad or anything but me and Sonya need really desperate help. (Stacey)

Stacey was a surprisingly self-aware child who had some understanding of how traditional, repetitive textbook exercises and exposing, whole-class questioning helped to position her at the bottom of the class. Whatever the impact of schools and teachers, we know from research that there are gender and social-class effects that cause children at different ages to respond differently to school mathematics. I will return to these briefly in the next chapter.

Contrast Stacey's experience with that of her peer, Edward. Despite being in the same class for the first six years of his school life he had somehow developed a very different view of his mathematics education. He ascribed value to his mathematics learning and described how he would regularly discuss mathematical problems with his dad, the apparent reason for this being his father's intention that he get into the local private school for boys. Edward's mathematical ability was not better than many of his peers but his family had particular aspirations and were well informed about the importance of mathematics in fulfilling their ambitions. They understood the value of some forms of knowledge over others in particular contexts. Moreover, Edward had the requisite language and cultural resources to talk about mathematics with apparent interest. His getting into that school was much more about his cultural and linguistic wealth than his self-designated mathematical skill.

Teachers on one of our Master's degree programmes have used a case study approach to explore what lies behind the attitudes and attainment of some of their students. Their case reports are very striking and really do get you thinking about how much life history and social circumstances influence mathematical progress. What you do with that knowledge is a challenge, but one worth thinking about. Better that than ignoring the very real links between life circumstances and mathematical learning.

MATHEMATICS LEARNING AS A SOCIAL PRACTICE

Mathematics education is intertwined with complex cultural and social processes at each phase of young people's learning. We know how language tends to disadvantage and filter out some learners of mathematics (Zevenbergen, 2001), how the UK national Key Stage tests also disadvantage certain social groups (Cooper and Dunne, 2000), and so on. Put together, this knowledge paints a bleak picture of the ways in which mathematics education becomes a gatekeeper to future opportunities. But are these effects present in all disciplines or are they peculiar to mathematics education? There is no doubt that from a sociological point of view many of these factors are generic to schooling. However, what we are interested in here is how these factors play out in the context of mathematics education.

At the end of compulsory schooling these various social factors impact upon patterns of enrolment to, and attainment in, AS and A2 mathematics courses. These trends did not go unnoticed as enrolment on degree-level mathematics courses (and the other STEM subjects) declined in the last decade of the twentieth century (see Tikly and Wolf, 2000a for an analysis of mathematics education at the turn of the millennium). The Royal Society expressed their concern about this, and the media, who rarely miss an opportunity to highlight the apparent problems of mathematics education, also made much of the trend. However, it does not take a learned society or media coverage to convince people of the belief that school mathematics is in some sense in a state of crisis – for it seems this popular belief has existed for some time and just refuses to go away (see the comments in the Cockcroft report, 1982, for example).

It would seem that to many school students, mathematics is one of those subjects that has to be endured. It is not the only curriculum subject that provokes such a response from children, but it does seem to stand out. Children's stereotypical images of mathematics teachers are not terribly flattering. Why is this, is there any truth in them, and how have teachers of mathematics come to have this particular modern-day image? One beginning teacher recently wrote about his experiences of learning mathematics, reporting that four out of five of his teachers were strict. He did not elucidate on the extent to which this personality trait influenced the style of teaching. Is this characteristic more common in mathematics teachers and, if so, is it desirable or possible to change this? An Australian colleague related how children with whom she had worked considered their mathematics teachers to take themselves (and their subject) far too seriously. Is that the same in the UK; in the school in which you teach? Maybe this is because we consider our subject to be so important – even though most mathematics teachers (unlike many other teachers) rarely engage with their subject outside of their work, or know much about how it is used in the world around them.

Many of the beginning teachers with whom I have worked identify their coming to like mathematics with a realization that they were ahead of many of their peers. This brings confidence and a self-assurance that is about distinction, of being 'better than'. For example,

> I have always enjoyed doing Mathematics since I became aware that I was good at the subject ... I found it very satisfying to be able to solve the problems and then get it right. I was also able to share my experiences with other students who had been unable to do the homework ... I loved the whole structured approach to mathematics and being able to solve the problems in a logical manner. This enjoyment of the subject was consolidated in the 6th form when I began to realize that others struggled with the subject and I was able to help out. (Peter)

This is not necessarily a problem but might become an issue if current teaching practice reproduces this response whereby only a small fraction of students can feel good about their mathematics learning.

Returning to Edward, he too had something to say about the role of ranking in mathematics assessment:

Edward:	I didn't do too well in the test about mathematics last time I only got 35 out of 45 and I was quite disappointed about that ... I think it was the nerves 'cause I couldn't really remember doing a proper test before.
Andy:	So were you disappointed because you got 35 out of 45 or because other people got more than you?
Edward:	Both.
Andy:	If you had got the top mark with 35 out of 45 would that have been good?
Edward:	Mmm, I would have felt better.
Andy:	So it's not only about how much you got but who you did better than?
Edward:	Yeah I suppose.
Andy:	Who do you want to be as good as?
Edward:	I want to be as good as Matt 'cause today we finished mathematics more or less exactly the same time so we're always you know ... top.

Unlike his peer – Stacey – who positioned herself as 'dumbest in the class', Edward was continually working to be at the other end of the ranking. Although Peter is some 30 years older than Edward, the same principle can be seen in their mathematical biographies. During the three decades that have elapsed since Peter left primary school there have been considerable changes in curriculum, pedagogy and assessment. Yet despite the changes there is something about mathematics and its role in the curriculum that has changed little over this time.

The Teaching 2020 project at the Department for Education and Skills (DfES) sought to imagine what schools might be like for the next generation of learners. You might like to think about this and consider what mathematics will be needed by future citizens and how school curricula and pedagogy might develop to meet this change. In thinking ahead in this way your focus should be on upon the mathematics needed to function in a range of social roles, rather than in mathematics classrooms. This is not an easy task. Indeed, this book is merely exploring the question of what mathematics learners need now and that is far from straightforward, without thinking 15 years ahead.

MATHEMATICS LEARNING AS A POLITICIZED PRACTICE

So if mathematics is of such social and cultural importance we need to consider what mathematics should be learnt in school and in what ways it should be taught. Hopefully, you have already thought about this in responding to the questions posed at the outset of Part I of this book. You might also have explored this when you started your teacher education programme but then have settled into the routines of teaching the National Curriculum, probably informed by some textbook scheme or other departmental traditions. Whatever position you are in as a teacher it is still worth asking yourself, 'Why do we teach the mathematics that we teach?' and 'What is the best way to teach what we teach?'

These complex questions have been debated over many decades and have been the focus of large-scale, expensive policy programmes in recent years in the UK. But what politics lies behind the current curriculum? The success of these expensive initiatives is a moot point (Brown et al., 2003) and certainly goes nowhere near the more radical rethink of curriculum that could be considered. Referring to similar reform processes in the USA, it has been suggested that 'true reform … may require doing something not better but different' (Kilpatrick and Stanic, 1995: 15). The word 'reform' signals a political intent here in England but the sense of this US view is very clear; we need to think outside the box of current curriculum trajectory in order to develop an alternative vision for mathematics education in England. I am not the first, nor will I be the last to argue this. As the French essayist Andre Gide has asserted, 'everything that needs to be said has already been said. But since no one was listening, everything must be said again' (a rather apt quote for some lessons I have taught!). So, it is important for us to keep exploring these fundamental questions about curriculum and pedagogy, whether we feel powerless to effect change or not. This is particularly so in the era of global and social upheaval that has been called the information(al) age or know-ledge society. Technology is shaping our everyday experiences and although information and communication technology (ICT) has not yet had the impact upon school education that had been predicted, there are still many who expect traditional learning to be transformed by the arrival of increasingly powerful mobile and web-based technologies.

What mathematical knowledge is important now and will be necessary in the future, and in what ways should learners engage with it? We need to be clear that the priorities of mathematics educators and teachers are different from those of professional mathematicians in the academy or industry and commerce. We also need to acknowledge that the politics of knowledge has ensured, historically, that the school curriculum has been heavily influenced by those powerful groups.

Whilst acknowledging that mathematics educators might take multiple standpoints on curriculum and pedagogy, and that these will be different again from policy-makers and professional mathematicians, there is something to be learnt from the latter. It is interesting that of the five quotes in the mathematics NC that offer some explanation of the nature of the subject, all come from mathematicians and academics; hardly representative of the range of users of mathematics![1] Unless of course these represent the intended beneficiaries of school mathematics education – those for whom mathematics will be strongly related to their future careers. However, even though their views are probably irrelevant to most learners of school mathematics, there are interesting contrasts to make between those who do mathematics for a living and those who have mathematics done to them in school. One of these five mathematicians, Andrew Wiles, celebrated for his proof of Fermat's last theorem, describes elsewhere his work like this:

> I never use a computer … l scribble … l do doodles. I start trying to find patterns. I'm doing calculations which try to explain some little piece of mathematics and I'm trying to fit it in with some previous broad conceptual understanding of

some branch of mathematics. Sometimes that will involve going and looking in a book to see how it's done; sometimes it's a question of modifying something a bit; sometimes doing a little calculation and sometimes you realize that nothing that's ever been done before is of any use at all and you just have to find something completely new and it's a mystery where it comes from ... (Andrew Wiles, BBC Horizon)

This is not an approach that has been adopted in the National Numeracy Strategy. Whether or not this kind of mathematical practice is typical of professional mathematicians I cannot say, but what I do know is that this kind of exploratory mathematical work is not a common experience for many children in school. This mathematician is an 'explorer' in an unknown and unpredictable landscape, rather than a 'ladder-climber' ascending predetermined, equally spaced NC rungs! What children experience in schools is in some ways a second-hand mathematical history, with little purpose or rationale given. It is the rehearsal of a basic grammar but is not a lived language. It is often received in the same way in which I experienced school history – an uninspiring set of dates and 'facts' to be learnt. But where languages in school have become less formal, and where history is more subjective and contested, mathematics has remained stuck in formality, abstraction and irrelevance. Many children are *trained* to do mathematical calculations rather that being *educated* to think mathematically. This discourse of training is something that has crept insidiously into teacher education as well and was the root of David's earlier criticism of his PGCE course: he wanted to be told; instead he learnt how to think! Philip Davis (1993: 191) made use of similar metaphors when he wrote:

> If mathematics is a language, it is time to put an end to an over concentration on its grammar and to study the 'literature' that mathematics has created and to interpret that literature. If mathematics is a logico-mechanism of a sort, then just as very few of us actually learn how to construct an automobile carburettor, but many of us take instruction in driving, so we must teach how to 'drive' mathematically and to *interpret what it means when we have been driven mathematically in a certain manner.* (original emphasis)

Although Andrew Wiles claims never to use a computer, this could well be due to the fact that he does not carry out repeated algorithmic calculations; he is not an automata or human computer, which is what many children in school mathematics are being trained to become. Mathematics is about much more than algorithms, so it seems sensible to revise the curriculum alongside the emergence of ubiquitous calculating machines that are much better at those kinds of tasks than us humans. However, traditionalists have been reluctant to rescind paper-and-pencil methods. Such arguments are not educational alone but become politicized in a complex and far from transparent way.

Consider another political dimension of mathematics learning. Nel Noddings (2004) suggested that the mathematics classrooms should become more politicized, with the children themselves negotiating curriculum and pedagogy. This would be a radical departure for most mathematics classrooms in England. She builds her argument on the work of Paolo Friere (for example, 1972) and John Dewey (for example, 1916) and offers an attractive alternative view of the mathematics classroom. However, her model is predicated upon a different kind of professionalism and school culture. By contrast, if you teach in an English state school it is more than likely that you are quite constrained by a centralized curriculum and preferred pedagogy. Perhaps you have become so used to how the mandated curriculum and pedagogic 'guidance' of the National Framework for Mathematics shapes the day-to-day mathematical learning experiences of children that you no longer question what happens in classrooms. Moreover, these 'strategies' are policed by Ofsted and the network of consultants (many of whom seem, in my experience, to be incapable or unwilling to see any fault with the costly system of surveillance and control of which they are a part). This all contributes to what has been described as the deprofessionaliza-tion of teachers' work. Gradually we are becoming a generation of teachers that do not have the motivation or know-how to question and critique the system in which we find ourselves. I hope that in reading this book you agree that these are important issues and are worth discussing. The notion of a crit-ical mathematics education is one to which I will return.

Another benefit of a more democratic approach was highlighted by Edmonds and Ball (1988: 128) when they asserted that 'the only way to make mathematics relevant to pupils who study it is to involve them in deciding what they want to learn and how they want to learn it'. Unfortunately, but understandably, this is a rare practice in the many schools mathematics departments with which I am familiar.

Questions

In your experience of school mathematics teaching how predictable are class-room teaching and learning styles? How often do teachers make choices about the curriculum and how much freedom and creativity is brought to bear on lessons? In order to answer these questions you will need to consider carefully all of the *normal* things that take place – why do these things happen and how do they benefit mathematical thinking and learning?

Could Andrew Wiles work in these classrooms? Does anyone discover or invent new (for them) mathematics?

How political/democratic are these classrooms and in what ways do they contribute to the education of future citizens?

MATHEMATICS LEARNING, CULTURE AND THE MEDIA

What is the role of mathematics in the general education of today's young citizen? Considering this question is one of the broad aims of the book, and I am of course assuming that mathematics education should, as a priority, be serving this aim. Your beliefs about the purposes of schooling and of mathematics education will clearly have a bearing upon your classroom pedagogy. Much research suggests that teachers' beliefs about the nature of mathematics and how it is best learnt are importantly related to their classroom practices, albeit in a rather untidy way (for example, Cooney and Shealy, 1997; Richardson, 1996; Schoenfeld, 2002; Thompson, 1992). Throughout this book you will reflect upon your own beliefs about mathematics education, recognizing that at times they will be contradictory to mine and to those of your colleagues. You might return to the questions posed at the outset of Part I and reconsider them as you proceed through these chapters.

It is not simply, or even primarily, the beliefs of teachers that have shaped the curriculum. Politicians and professional users and creators of mathematics have also played a key role. At this point we should also acknowledge that another, much larger, group has considerable influence (albeit a diffuse one [Noyes, 2004a]) and that is the general public. Public images of mathematics, mathematics education, mathematics teachers are longstanding. These images are non-homogenous but do have some recurring characteristics (Sam, 2002). So it is generally acceptable to be able to claim to be non-mathematical or innumerate but socially far less acceptable to claim to be illiterate. This is not a new view: 'most people are so frightened of the name of mathematics that they are ready, quite unaffectedly, to exaggerate their own mathematical stupidity' (Hardy, 1941). If Hardy was right, how does such a fear of mathematics come about?

Despite the fact that we know from the Basic Skills Agency report (Bynner and Parsons, 1997) that poor numeracy (we will consider this term in Chapter 4) is more closely related to poverty than poor literacy, negative attitudes to mathematics continue. Although much evidence of society's antipathy towards mathematics is anecdotal, it somehow seems to have become deeply embedded in our collective cultural psyche.

Images of mathematics and mathematicians are writ large in well-known films such as *Good Will Hunting*, *A Beautiful Mind* and more recently *Proof*. Not only do these films perpetuate particular notions of masculinity (Mendick, 2004), but mathematical genius is intermingled with eccentricity at best, and serious mental illness at worst. Rarely is the mathematician a balanced, healthy individual, and these films are more about the lives of the mathematicians than the work that they did.

When it comes to the print and news media the headlines and scare stories often do little to ameliorate the poor image of mathematics. The British Broadcasting Corporation (BBC) has reported on the publication of the Smith report (2004) as an 'action plan to rescue mathematics' (BBC News, 4 February 2004); on a survey reporting over 50 per cent of 16–18-year-old 'students struggling at mathematics' (BBC News, 2 May 2005a); on 'the secret shame of maths teachers' (2 September 1999) in primary schools; and on mathematics being stuck in a 'spiral of decline' (28 June 2005b). Meanwhile, in the *Guardian* newspaper Linda Nordling prefaced her report on the scarcity of skilled mathematics graduates suitable for research posts with 'maths was never the most popular subject at school' (*Guardian*, 5 July 2005a). So what general impression should we get of the state of mathematics education? Not a positive one but, rather, a sense that the discipline is in trouble.

Simon Singh is a 'champion' of mathematics yet his interpretation of the rationale for the aforementioned films is that 'Hollywood thinks mathematics is sexy' (*Guardian*, 24 October 2005b). Surely a more critical view is needed where the impact of such 'role models' is questioned. He goes on to suggest, rather melodramatically, that:

> mathematics in Britain could become extinct over the next few decades because fewer people are studying mathematics as each year passes, which means there will be fewer people who can teach it, so even fewer will be able to study it and eventually the tradition of Brits doing clever things with numbers will disappear forever.

His argument is supported by the evidence of declining numbers taking A level mathematics in recent decades. In the same press article Singh tells us that this should concern us because 'the repercussions on the UK economy will be enormous as we fail to find enough people with the skills who can help Britain compete in the information age'. The proposed solution is to have a sufficiently qualified and trained new generation of mathematics teachers. Of course the supply and education of mathematics teachers is important, but to simplify the problem to this one issue and to overlook the issues of curriculum and pedagogy that we are thinking about here will not get us far. No doubt the daily press is not the place to enter into such discussion, but at the same time we need to be aware that this is the level of debate to which young people's parents are exposed.

Having sounded a rather negative tone, there are examples of the widening debate called for by mathematicians (whose concerns are usually for those elite students who will fill their courses and follow in their mathematical footsteps). This debate has included the questioning of compulsory mathematics: should all young people be required to study GCSE mathematics? Why? Terry Bladon's comments on this matter of removing mathematics from the core curriculum from age 14, were widely and sympathetically reported (for example, BBC News, 21 April 2003). For some time academics have added to this debate in the national press on more philosophical grounds (for example, BBC News, 3 October 2000). There is an important discussion that needs to take place and is happening in part. The debate revolves around the usefulness of mathematics and its importance for the general education of teenage students, which is an important matter. But strangely, the curriculum and its associated pedagogies, assessment regimes and resource supports are not questioned. Perhaps such drastic solutions would not need to be debated if the curriculum and underpinning pedagogic rationale were instead the focus of discussion.

MATHEMATICS LEARNING FOR OPPORTUNITY

The problem with suggesting that not all students continue with mathematics until the end of their schooling is that currently this would prohibit their access to the learning and life opportunities which are predicated upon attaining a GCSE grade C or above. So despite society's antipathy towards mathematics there is the acknowledgement that somehow mathematics has power, or rather, success in school mathematics has the power to change one's future life trajectory. This is primarily at the level of the individual, whose GCSE C grade or above allows him or her into many further and higher education opportunities or who with an A level can apparently command greater earning power.

I am not convinced that the NC or other recent mathematics education policy has done much to reduce the negative perception of mathematics held by many children and adults. The mantra of raising standards that has been the hallmark of education policy in recent years has not improved things. Slightly higher grades, and any associated feeling of success, might have had an impact on attitudes but the evidence suggests that mathematics is still considered to be harder than other subjects. Why this should be remains a mystery but surely relates to the politics of knowledge, to the idea that somehow mathematical and/or scientific knowledge is loftier.

So, mathematics education is far from being sorted. Moreover the problems go deeper than image. In trying to address the 'crisis', the Smith report (2004) has highlighted possible directions for the development of mathematics education. Many of these are concerned with shoring up the current system. The shortage of teachers is a central concern, as is the content of the curriculum. However, sadly, what is lacking in the report is a more critical and considered view on the purpose of school education and of the mathematics curriculum.

More pertinent to the direction of the discussion here is the work of critical mathematics educators like Eric Gutstein (2006). In his book, *Reading and Writing the World with Mathematics*, he explains that the acquisition of mathematical power through a 'pedagogy of access' is only one facet of a socially just mathematics curriculum. There is a need to accompany this with a 'pedagogy of dissent' by which he means those practices which are concerned with understanding the place and power of mathematics in society and giving all learners the skills to use their mathematics as engaged citizens. I referred to the National Curriculum earlier and its assertion that mathematics might be used to 'understand and change the world'. This is precisely what Gutstein is advocating is and an important theme of the following chapters. However, I suspect that Gutstein and the research mathematicians quoted in the NC might have slightly different takes on what this might mean!

SUMMARY

In this chapter I have briefly surveyed the landscape of mathematics education and have highlighted some of the particular problems and features that will be explored in greater depth through the rest of the book. It should be clear that the issues which most concern me are those relating to the political purposes and related pedagogies of school mathematics. I use the word 'political' in a broad sense here, recognizing that the school curriculum is contested by powerful groups, in accordance with their own interests. School students do not get a say in what they should learn and, generally speaking, the powerful groups that do get to influence curriculum content are those that have already benefited from it. We should be concerned for those students who will never, under the current regime, see how mathematics might be a powerful tool with which to understand and change the world. These students are not only those who currently fail to meet the arbitrary required grade C standard but the many that do actually achieve this, but for whom it was purely an educational hoop-jumping exercise. Before proceeding you might consider the following questions.

Questions

How important is it to you that school mathematics engages with real issues of relevance to learners?

- To what extent do you do this already?
- Can you find examples of apparently relevant mathematics that is actually unrealistic?

What might it mean to use mathematics to understand and change the world?

- Can you think of some examples?
- How, if at all, do mathematics lessons in your school enable learners to develop the knowledge, skills and understanding that will make this happen?

KEY TEXTS

The three texts listed below have different national contexts (the USA, Germany and the UK) and audiences. The authors have very different roles and relationships to mathematics. You might not want to read these at this stage and I will refer to the first two in more depth during the later chapters. The Smith report is more pertinent to mathematics teachers in the UK and the executive summary provides an outline of the main recommendations that are already impacting upon the learning and teaching of mathematics in schools and colleges.

Smith, A. (2004) *Making Mathematics Count*. London: HMSO.
Every teacher will have heard of the Smith report but it is worth reading, as the implications for teachers of mathematics are considerable. It is available, or can be purchased, online. Even a read of the executive summary would be informative.

Gutstein, E. (2006) *Reading and Writing the World with Mathematics: Toward a Pedagogy for Social Justice.* New York: Routledge.
This book is a semi-autobiographical account of Gutstein's work with disadvantaged students in Chicago. He describes the political nature of his mathematics teaching and how his pedagogy has increased motivation for many of his students. There are descriptions of the kinds of tasks that he used to enable the students to learn to 'read and write the world' mathematically. It is easy to read and I would encourage you to read it – even if you cannot agree with everything that Gutstein advocates.

Heymann, H.W. (2003) *Why Teach Mathematics: A Focus on General Education.* Dordrecht: Kluwer.
This thesis is a thorough, thought-provoking vision for development of German mathematics education, with a lot that is relevant for the UK. Although from a different political tradition to Gutstein, many of the ideas complement one another as Heymann asks questions about the usefulness of secondary mathematics. The cost of the book is prohibitive, but if you are seriously interested in these issues it is worth borrowing.

NOTE

1 The quote from Professor Robert Worcester, Chairman of the Market and Opinion Research Institute (MORI), is of relevance here: 'if you want to take part in tomorrow's world, you'll need mathematics and statistics just as much as grammar and syntax' (NC: p. 15).

WHO DOES MATHEMATICS?

The quick answer to the title question is 'everyone'. Perhaps more interesting questions then are 'Who does mathematics well?', or 'Which groups are relatively successful in mathematics?' This chapter will briefly explore these questions.

We will also examine retention and engagement patterns of students in post-compulsory mathematics education. Throughout the 1990s a decreasing number of students chose to study mathematics beyond GCSE, but just who stays and who goes at this critical transition point? Although we do not have detailed answers to some of these questions, this chapter will get you thinking about patterns of attainment and engagement in your own school.

Throughout the chapter there are questions that will support your investigations into who is doing what mathematics in your school. This might not be as easy as it would at first appear because the data that you require might not be easily accessible. Perhaps the more important issue is what you do with the knowledge of these patterns. Can and should you try and disrupt these or is that just the way it is?

WHO DOES WHAT MATHEMATICS?

Whilst we know that many learners are not well served by their mathematics education, both in terms of the final outcomes and life opportunities it affords them, and in the actual learning processes in the classroom, we know that this is not the case for all learners. Many school students do enjoy their mathematics lessons and choose to continue studying the subject beyond their compulsory schooling.

Across the attainment spectrum learners engage in different kinds of mathematics with different underlying principles and purposes. I will discuss this in more detail in the next chapter but, very simply, the notions of numeracy, whether part of a National Strategy or a Key Skills programme, and functional mathematics are different in focus from A level Further Mathematics, for example. So to ask 'Who does mathematics?' runs the risk of missing a related but important issue, namely, 'And what mathematics do they do?' You might like to think about the differences between the high- and low-attaining groups that you teach (assuming they are ability groups). What kind of content, resources and pedagogy do they experience and what expectations do you have of them? For example, there is a current fad of teachers using the notion of learning styles to argue that lower-attaining groups need more 'kinaesthetic' work. Why might this be a problem? What assumptions have been made in coming to this view, and are they right? In addition, the current policy for supporting 'gifted and talented' learners has sometimes meant that supposedly 'gifted' learners get an enriched experience of mathematics. Surely, if it is possible to enrich the mathematical learning experience then all learners should benefit. Many of these features of the mathematics learning landscape are peculiar to England (and to varying extents the UK) and Alison Wolf (2000) draws our attention to the differences between what happens here and in many other parts of the world.

As well as looking at some patterns of attainment and retention in mathematical study, you will also consider the differential success of various groups. How much do school processes and classroom practices contribute to these patterns of engagement and attainment? We cannot do much in the context of this chapter and you might think that this look at some of the data raises more questions than it answers. This is true, and I think that because the data here is from national cohorts it is of limited use to you in your schools, where the patterns of attainment and engagement might well be very different. So what is important is an inquiring approach to what is happening in the school in which you are currently working. What is happening and why? Moreover, what could and should you and your colleagues do about it? This distinction between the global and the local is also something that would apply if you were using pupil perspectives to improve their learning experience. You can read all about what children think of learning mathematics nationally and it have little affect – we can all convince ourselves that the insightful critiques of young people do not apply to us. However, if your classes appraise their experiences of school and mathematics then it is much more difficult not to act in response. So it is important in the context of this chapter that you look carefully at the particular patterns in your own school and classroom.

We do know quite a lot about some aspects of engagement and attainment patterns, for example, males/females at AS and A level. We also know how social factors (including the setting of children in school) can affect attainment and engagement (for example, Boaler, 1997; Boaler et al., 1998; Fennema and Leder, 1990; Walkerdine, 1998). Indeed, gender analyses are relatively straightforward as much of the data available records this simple division. The problem, of course, is that young people's identities are more complex than male/female and an understanding based solely on gender is rather partial. So if you wanted to include the impact of social groups, say ethnic heritage or social class, the issues become far more complex. Unfortunately these social dimensions probably have a greater impact upon learner progress in mathematics, so you might like to explore these in your own context, perhaps within one class or year group. Some of the questions in this chapter will help you to do this.

Before continuing with this chapter

Consider the school in which you are now working, or one with which you are familiar:

- What kind of community does it serve? What funds of mathematical knowledge do you think various groups in this community have?
- How are children grouped for mathematics? Is there any patterning across the age and ability range? Is there equal representation of male/female, ethnic groups and so on in these groups? How, if at all, does this differ at ages 11, 15, 18?
- To what extent are these age groups taught in different ways? What is the rationale for this difference?

If you are interested in this kind of analysis of engagement and attainment in mathematics you might like to make use of data from the Neighbourhood Statistics website (www.neighbourhood.statistics.gov.uk) or www.upmystreet.com in relation to the first question. The first of these provides a rich source of census level data at various levels that would enable you to understand something of the school catchment. UpMyStreet is based more upon market research data but is also very helpful in providing some kind of profile of the school's catchment area.

THE CLASS OF 2001

In order to explore some of the issues let us consider the national cohort of GCSE students that completed their mathematical studies in 2001 (Figure 2.1). This might include you. The charts included here record their progress through school. In 1996 they were one of the early groups to complete the mandatory national tests at age 11. Based on an extensive quantitative study of children's responses to two categories of question on the national tests (realistic and esoteric) Cooper and Dunne (2000) have argued that children from lower socio-economic categories are relatively disadvantaged. Children from the middle classes (this division is an oversimplification but helps to make the point) have acquired the forms of language and cultural knowledge needed to negotiate school, and more specifically these tests, successfully. Realistic questions are normally not realistic at all, and if the student reads this pseudo-realism too literally (as is more likely the case with children from lower socio-economic groups) they generate sensible, but mathematically unacceptable, solutions. The research indicated that when magnified over large cohorts this can have a significant impact upon selection patterns at the primary–secondary interface. That should not be a problem though because we generally do not have selection at age 11 – well not officially! However, many of the schools I visit do select, by ability grouping, either upon arrival at the secondary school or shortly thereafter.

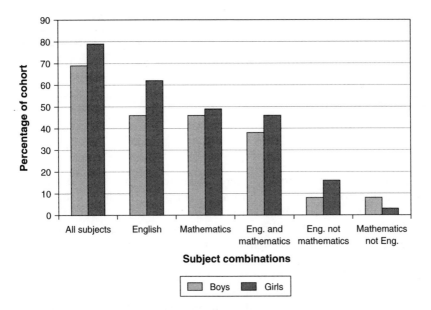

FIGURE 2.1: GCSE A*–C grades in 2001 cohort

Three years later in 1999 this cohort completed their compulsory national tests at age 14, the end of Key Stage 3. Fortunately this cohort did not have to endure the additional 'progress tests' that now contribute to English schoolchildren being some of the most (over)assessed in the world. The net effect of these kinds of national tests, when combined with common practice of ability grouping (setting), is that some groups of children are gradually filtered up/down through the ranking of test scores. One local teacher recently pointed out that all her bottom group were on the free school meals register (FSM) whereas only a few of the top group were marked by this default indicator of low socio-economic status. Although social-class effects are not the only influence upon mathematical success (gender, being more visible and therefore easier to measure, has received considerable attention) it remains the key predictor of school success (Connolly, 2006).

During their school careers the general attainment of girls is higher than that of boys, and by the end of year 11 the difference between boys and girls is maintained. However, an important distinction emerges in patterns of attainment. It is not simply that girls outperform boys across the subjects, as there is a notable difference between English and mathematics. The reported data includes these figures and, although they do not tell us about how other subject combinations work, they do give us an insight into how progress to this point might impact upon the first post-compulsory choices for continued mathematical study.

What is particularly interesting in Figure 2.1 is the combination of English and mathematics. This has particular relevance for the participation rates of boys and girls in different kinds of further and higher education as the role

TABLE 2.1   Attained A2 grades for 2001 GCSE cohort completing A2 in 2003

	A	B	C	D	E	TOTAL Entries
Male	10,347	5,425	4,465	3,372	2,333	27,238
Female	6,388	3,544	2,481	1,804	952	16,625

Source: DfES.

of English and mathematics as prerequisites for further study is still very important in some areas. The fifth and sixth pairs of columns shows how there are twice as many girls as there are boys attaining grade C or above in English but not in mathematics, which you might expect given the difference in grade C attainment for English and mathematics. If decisions regarding post-16 choices are made partly in relation to subject confidence, then this data suggests this might not be as great for girls in mathematics as it is in English. The data presented is Figure 2.1 does not exactly tell us this, but it fits with what we know about the gendered nature of school mathematics whereby despite the relative success of girls' their engagement in, and enjoyment of, mathematics does not appear to have increased.

So now let us see how this 2001 cohort gets on when they opt for AS courses and when they reach their A level examinations. The full data from 2003 excludes some that retook modules and so completed later in 2004 and includes students from the 2002 A2 cohort that completed a year late in 2003 (Table 2.1). It is difficult to tease out this data so I have simply worked with those students who took two years from 2001 to 2003.[1]

The first thing that is clear is the significantly smaller number of female candidates – there has been a huge opt-out for girls compared with boys. What also seems to have happened (see Figures 2.2 and 2.3) is that a smaller proportion of the girls have attained the lower grades. This might be because they have worked harder or that more of them made choices based upon their likelihood of success (the reasons are no doubt more complex than both of these ideas).

This sharp drop from A to B grades might have a simple cause, namely, that students are actively deterred from studying A level if they have not demonstrated certain levels of attainment (normally grade B) at GCSE (Mendick, 2005). This is all tied up with the idea that mathematics is hard; the net result is a profile like the above which could be interpreted as mathematics A level students doing particularly well (and so they must be clever) because they got lots of A grades. This might help to explain why having an A level in mathematics apparently leads to higher career earnings (Wolf, 2002) because the selection process to A level is selective. Perhaps the higher earnings argument is not what it seems. My analysis here is nowhere near detailed enough so I present these graphs with some caution. However, the data do indicate that something significant has happened at the transition from GCSE to A level for this cohort.

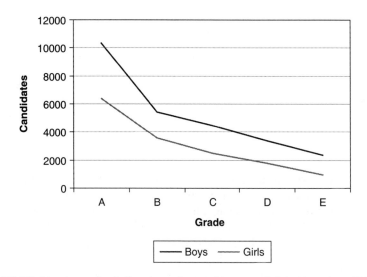

FIGURE 2.2 Numbers of male/female students achieving each A level grade in 2003 cohort
Source: DfES.

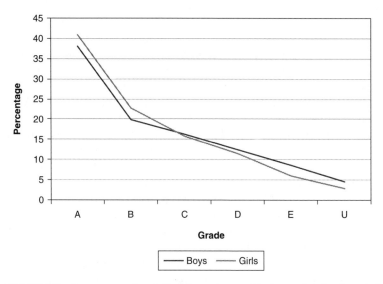

FIGURE 2.3   Percentage of male/female students achieving each A level grade in 2003 cohort
Source: DfES.

It is interesting to compare the A level attainment pattern of our focus cohort completing in 2003 (post-Curriculum 2000) with that of five years previously (1998) (pre-Curriculum 2000). See Table 2.2.

What does this tell us? That fewer students completed an A level (in two years) in 2003 than five years earlier but that the proportion of top grades

TABLE 2.2   Change in GCE A level mathematics attainment 1998/2003

		A	B	C	D	E	TOTAL Entries
2003	Male	10,347	5,425	4,465	3,372	2,333	27,238
	Female	6,388	3,544	2,481	1,804	952	16,625
1998	Male	10,474	6,580	5,774	5,020	3,935	35,524
	Female	5,521	4,162	3,500	2,688	1,874	19,464

Source: DfES.

was greater. Owing to the turbulence that was caused by the introduction of AS/2 system in 2000 is it not worth reading too much into this, but the change is marked. The following outline statistics highlight the impact of the 2000 changes. In 1998 13 per cent of the cohort did not achieve an A–E grade. When the new AS first appeared, of around 55,000 candidates entered for the examination a staggering 27 per cent did not pass. This helps to explain the difference. Unfortunately this data tells us very little about differences across ethnic and social-class groups.

In the earlier of the two years, 1998, the pattern of attainment across schools was as shown in Figure 2.4. Although the same data is not readily available for 2003, we might guess that the pattern of attainment between school types is not markedly different. However, it would be interesting to know how the patterns of engagement and attainment have changed over the last 10 years, and at a more detailed level than offered by this data. This might tell us whether the changes in recruitment to, and attainment in, A level mathematics are the same in all schools or whether in fact the changes cloak a narrowing of participation in some areas more than in others. What proportion of students attaining A/B grades at GCSE proceed to study mathematics at A level in your school? This is an issue that might be worth discussing with colleagues who work in a variety of schools across a region. If there are any differences what reasons might be given for this variation?

We have been looking at the 2003 A2 cohort, yet this was only the second cohort of students to complete the newly styled examinations, having done AS in the previous year. They had opted for mathematics before the impact of the Curriculum 2000 changes described above was fully known. So, compared to the 13 per cent of candidates who did not pass their A level in 1998, in 2003 the figure had dropped to less than 5 per cent of the cohort with many pulling out following unsuccessful completion of the AS year.

Questions

If you have data available relating to the GSCE/A level transition what can you learn from the patterns of engagement and attainment?

Do they match up with this national picture? If not, what reasons might you give for this?

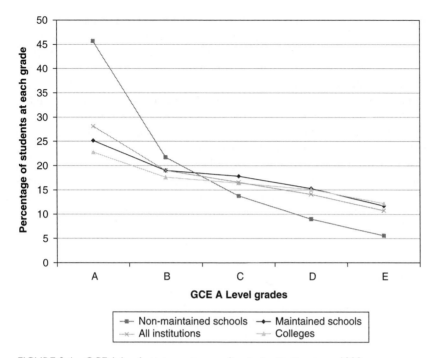

FIGURE 2.4   GCE A level attainment according to institution type, 1998

INVESTIGATING ENGAGEMENT AND ATTAINMENT

In the context of this chapter I only want to spend a very short amount of time considering how engagement and attainment in mathematics is patterned across the complex social categories of gender, ethnicity and social class. Each of these areas has been the subject of books and research papers and, if you are interested, there is a plethora of reading available (for example, Cooper and Dunne, 1998; Fennema and Leder, 1990; Kassem, 2001; Zevenbergen, 2001).

Of these three areas there has probably been the most attention given to gender issues (the data is readily available, as seen above) and some of the questions raised by the differential post-compulsory mathematical participation of boys and girls are relevant across all school phases. Research in gender and mathematics education uses a range of data and theoretical perspectives to explore the reasons why differences in boys' and girls' attainment and participation occur. Critiques of the masculinized historical development of mathematics have shown how this bias is played out in teaching and how it affects the views of girls (Mendick, 2005; Paechter, 2000).

Although much concern has been expressed about the engagement of girls in mathematics and related sciences, evidence from large-scale youth cohort studies makes clear that ethnicity and social class are far more significant indicators of general success. That does not mean to say that gender matters are unimportant – far from it. You need to understand those issues as well as understand how ethnicity, class, disability, and so on, impacts upon mathematical engagement and attainment. The exploration of gender issues in mathematics education is made possible by the wealth of statistical data collected each year on pupils. Derek Kassem (2001) explains that the opposite is true for understanding ethnic attainment, due to the relative lack of data available.

Perhaps the most difficult social category for teachers to understand and make sense of in relation to their teaching is social class. Social class does not exist in a fixed, objective sense, but rather is something that is done on an ongoing basis: we classify and are classified in an ongoing way. As mathematics teachers we do this too – all the time. You might like to reflect on the judgements you form of classes when you first meet them. How do you decide who is good at mathematics, or who is likely to be successful? From my work with teachers (Noyes, 2006a) I have suggested that teachers use five levels of data to classify, partly subconsciously, children and their mathematical potential:

1 Systemic – national test scores/levels and other assessment data
2 Historical – knowledge of older siblings and possibly parents
3 Academic – concerning work done in the classroom, and which is related to
4 Behaviour – concerning attitudes to work and people, and which is related to
5 Style – these are factors concerned with 'taste', for example, dress, manners, body language.

What particularly interested me in that study was how mathematics teachers formed opinions of young people's mathematical potential on the lower levels of style and behaviour that gradually proved to be quite influential for the learners.

Investigate these issues further

Consider one of the classes you teach. Can you discern any patterns of engagement or attainment in the class that relate to these social categories? This is easier to do with the more visible categories (gender and ethnicity) and more difficult to relate to social background. In order to do this you might use assessment records or video and analyse your teaching, if permissible in the school.

Do you think that your own practice, and that of the department, school and education system contributes to any such difference? In what ways?

Talk to some boys and girls studying mathematics at different times during their education. How do they describe their positive and negative views of mathematics?

Analyse school data on Key Stage test data to see whether there are any clear patterns.

One particular group that you might like to focus your attention upon are the 'quietly disaffected' in one of your classes; the ones that neither cause too much trouble nor display much enthusiasm for their mathematics (assuming that such a group exists of course). Nardi and Steward's (2003) research suggests that many of these pupils suffer from mathematics lessons being TIRED:

1 Tedious
2 Isolating
3 Rote learning
4 Elitist
5 Depersonalizing.

These five aspects of the typical mathematics experience result in considerable disaffection and disengagement. You might consider whether or not these categories are applicable in your own schools and classes. Also, in the context of this discussion, are there groups of children that are overrepresented in this quietly disaffected group.

ONE MATHEMATICS FOR ALL?

We have focused quite a bit in this chapter on the pattern of A level recruitment and attainment and, although this is, in some sense, of tangential interest, it has lead us into thinking about some of the issues surrounding who does mathematics in school. It has also highlighted the lack of quantitative evidence concerning the social patterning of engagement and attainment, although there is much research that is relevant to this discussion. Having spent some time looking at who is learning, you might like to consider at this point whether or not all learners should have access to the same school mathematics curriculum. Before proceeding try to answer the following questions:

Consider the children in the school in which you are working

What range of careers are they likely to end up doing? Do you know what the mathematical requirements are of these jobs?

To what extent, if at all, do you think the curriculum should aim to prepare learners for the professional groups identified above? Should this be a high priority for school mathematics?

What mathematics might these learners appreciate or find useful in the various areas of their lives? (This might be knowledge, skills or understanding.) Are the areas that you have identified appropriate for all learners?

So, what mathematics should all learners experience, understand and be able to use?

These are difficult questions to answer and you will be able to think through the implications of your answers in the following chapter and later in the book. There are those who have suggested that school mathematics is of little use to most students and so should not be part of the compulsory curriculum. Whilst this may be true, it is also the case that many professional people do use various kinds of mathematics in their daily work. Whether or not school mathematics is any kind of effective preparation is arguable.

The problem with arguing for the preparatory value of school mathematics (for whatever kind and level of application) is that we need to know whether or not the skills and knowledge and understanding developed in the classroom are transferable to, and indeed applicable in, other life contexts. This is an issue that has been explored by researchers, and the conclusion that we might draw from their analyses is that classroom mathematics is exactly that, mathematics for the classroom with limited applicability elsewhere. This makes redundant the question as to whether all pupils should experience the same curriculum content and takes us back to those bigger questions about the nature of teaching and learning mathematics, and schooling in general. Perhaps we would be better to think about the skills and processes that can be developed in mathematics lessons and then applied elsewhere.

SUMMARY

In this shorter chapter you have begun to consider patterns of mathematical engagement and attainment in young people. You have been invited to investigate how attainment is not random across society or in your school, but is patterned according to categories like gender, social class and ethnicity. These are not mutually exclusive groups and so the interactions are complex. However, doing some work in your school should help you to investigate engagement and attainment, and indeed whether the standard social groups provide helpful categories. You might decide that the variations are so complex that such approaches do not really help you to understand the issues. Of course, any superficial data collection and analysis will not give simple or causal explanations for patterns of engagement and attainment, so you will need to return to those principles of criticality mentioned in the introduction. Nevertheless, part of your professional role is to understand the nature of pupils' backgrounds and the impact that they have upon progress. To that end what is particularly important is that you develop a critical disposition to what you do as a teacher and in your department. How do these practices contribute to the differential success of various groups and what, if anything, might you do in order to disrupt these processes?

FURTHER READING

If you are interested in these social issues of engagement and attainment there is a wealth of material available and many sources are referenced in the other chapters of this book. Much of this was written with an academic audience in mind but should nevertheless give you some means of understanding the sociology of learning mathematics.

Cooper, B. and Dunne, M. (2000) *Assessing Children's Mathematical Knowledge: Social Class, Sex and Problem Solving*. Buckingham: Open University Press.

Gates, P. (ed.) (2001) *Issues in Mathematics Teaching*. London: RoutledgeFalmer.

Paechter, C. (2000) *Changing School Subjects: Power, Gender and Curriculum*. Buckingham: Open University Press.

Walkerdine, V. (1998) *Counting Girls Out: Girls and Mathematics*. London: Falmer Press.

NOTE

---

1 That is were 17 years of age at the start of the academic year.

'WHAT'S THE POINT OF DOING THIS?'

Having set the scene in the last two chapters we will now consider in more depth why we teach mathematics in the ways that we do. There is no single purpose for education or for school mathematics, but some ideals and groups have tended to exert greater influence over curriculum and pedagogy than others. These various purposes relate to different political and social views on the world but key influences have been made by those in society with relatively more power. So I suppose you might say that this chapter aims to raise your socio-political consciousness – not something that many mathematics teachers are concerned about in the context of their classroom teaching. However, I hope that by the end of the chapter you will see that understanding the politics of mathematics is very closely related to understanding why we teach what we teach.

As you read this chapter you should consider your own practices and those you have seen in schools, and reflect on the explicit and implicit purposes underpinning them.

A VEXING QUESTION

From the outset of my mathematics teaching career the question 'What's the point of doing this?' from pupils was perhaps the most vexing. It was one of those questions that my teacher education programme had not prepared me for and the more I considered the possible answers the more I realized that many of the reasons were not all that convincing, either to me or to the children I was teaching. My responses were often more concerned with the social and cultural roles of mathematics than with some intrinsic worth in the subject itself, although this is one good reason for mathematics being part of the curriculum. The suggestion by one colleague that as a teacher I was simply an *agent of the state* was troubling and something that I have wrestled with.

Some questions to consider whilst reading this chapter

To what extent do, or should, mathematics teachers have autonomy in their classrooms?

(Continued)

How free do you think teachers feel they are; in their planning, choice of resources and content, teaching and learning approaches, and so on?

What constrains the ways teachers teach? This will vary depending upon your experience and the school in which you are teaching.

Take some time to identify freedoms in, and constraints upon, your classroom practice as well as the sources and effects of such freedoms and constraints.

Should the teacher as an intellectual be engaged in practices that could be counter to the dominant political ideologies of the day? To what extent should teaching be subversive?

If, having read this book, you feel that there is good reason to question and challenge some of the dominant ideas about teaching and learning of mathematics, how should you go about it? This is a professional or even moral conundrum and the reason why mathematics teachers need to talk about these difficult questions that relate to the way mathematics is taught. Some beginning teachers (and teacher educators) with whom I have worked insist that teachers need to get the *basics* (not that there is anything basic about teaching) of their classroom practice established first before considering such matters but this is to put *the cart before the horse*. Practices and principles are dialectically related and need to develop together.

IS MATHEMATICS 'USEFUL FOR EVERYDAY LIFE'?

I have heard hundreds of beginning teachers express the view that 'mathematics is useful for everyday life' and then flounder when asked about the mathematics that they have used recently in their own everyday experiences. In fact the mathematics NC also makes this same point, but to what 'everyday life' are they referring. Such a view reminds me of the tale of the emperor's new clothes in which the emperor had been duped into thinking that his apparent nakedness actually appeared as fine clothes to every other eye. So it is with many mathematics teachers who continue to argue for the usefulness of mathematics in everyday life in contrast to the masses, in this case schoolchildren, who can see that this patently is not the case, or at least not in a simply understood way. So we have numerous textbooks and mathematics schemes that make extensive use of apparently real-life contexts where mathematics is used but we know that in reality what people actually do is quite different. This is partly because of the ways in which much classroom mathematics uses abstracted and simplified models of some reality but in detaching them from the complex social conditions in which they would normally be situated they become unreal.

Consider, for example the market-leading mathematics scheme in the UK at the start of the millennium. A quick survey of some of the real-life contexts in one of the texts raises some intriguing questions:

- Do people really pick single socks randomly from a drawer? (probability)
- Why would I be interested in calculating the long length of a triangular scarf if the lengths of the shorter sides are given; or the slope length of an old-fashioned tent if I know its width and height? Does the man cleaning the gutter really calculate whether his ladder is long enough? (Pythagoras)
- Would the girl really calculate the circumference of the lampshade she is making (note the gender stereotypes) in order to buy the right amount of braiding – surely a tape measure would be quicker? Or you could just buy a bit too much to be on the safe side! (circles) And who makes lampshades anyway?

I could go on to list a large number of contrived situations in which mathematics could be used. The problem is that there is no doubt some mathematical 'work' is being done in many of the situations in the textbook but it is far from being real. Try looking carefully in the text that your school uses and you will quickly see many such examples. The problem is that we have all been conditioned to think that these applications are realistic, so we tend to just go on perpetuating the myth, unquestioningly sticking by the authors' definitions of mathematical realism.

Research on adult workers' use of mathematics in the workplace shows that there is often a lot of complex mathematical activity taking place in such real-life contexts, but it is what might be termed 'situated' mathematics and not the same as 'school mathematics', which itself is largely only useful for that context. Often this is not advanced mathematics but it is being used in a flexible and sometimes sophisticated way. So the issue of the transferability of classroom knowledge is something that should be very important for teachers if they insist that mathematics is preparatory and functional.

HIDDEN MATHEMATICS

So there is a difference between what many teachers and textbooks perceive to be real-life mathematics and what people experience in their lives. In addition, where it might once have been the case that we needed to be able to use traditional algorithms to carry out certain calculations in everyday matters this is less so nowadays. This shift relates to the way in which mathematics has become so deeply embedded, complex and specialized in our everyday worlds that we do not always see it and would typically not understand even if we could. So it is not the case that there is no application of mathematics in life but the ways in which we encounter mathematics are changing. Of course one could still add up a shopping bill, subtract that 10 per cent discount, or calculate the best mobile phone deal. In reality such calculations are conducted by electronic devices such that there is not even the need to check change if paying electronically. I was recently quite satisfied that I had managed to turn purchasing a mobile phone into a mathematical problem, but I still ended up picking the one that I liked and was slim enough to fit into my pocket. Mathematical modelling in this case might have had some usefulness but needs to be combined with other ways of knowing, thinking and deciding. That is not to say that mathematics is unimportant or of no use but, rather, there is a disjunction between the traditional curriculum and the lived experiences of everyday citizens. So not only is mathematics increasingly embedded or hidden in everyday situations, but when we do some mathematizing of these daily situations the mathematics being used is mixed up with other processes of thought and action.

UNDERSTANDING PURPOSE IS OF PARAMOUNT IMPORTANCE!

The examples above are applications of classroom mathematics in life. Perhaps this is the wrong way around. If one wanted a utilitarian curriculum then looking first at the uses of mathematics would be better. This is what some have argued about the importance of understanding workplace applications of mathematics and is also the concern underpinning the recommendations in recent reports about mathematics and the 14–19 curriculum (DfES, 2004; Smith, 2004). However, that might be useful only if your overriding rationale for curriculum design were its usefulness, and here there begins to emerge some of the complexities of exploring this issue of curriculum. Skills and knowledge that might be useful for the well-educated workforce in the future economy are not necessarily the same as those demanded by academia. In addition, neither of these two are, as I will argue, what is needed for the general education of a future citizenry. So the question 'What's the point of doing this?' is of fundamental importance and requires teachers and others involved in mathematics education, either directly or at distance, to review what the curriculum has been for; who it has served. This might explain in a more helpful way the current landscape of UK mathematics education. It is also the starting point for challenging the dominant curriculum that has changed little in form and structure over decades.

SETTING MATHEMATICS TRAJECTORIES

In Chapter 1 we looked at how mathematics in school has a social role of gatekeeper, allowing some to pass through to future opportunity whilst closing others out. That idea is focused on the attainment of GCSE grade C, but this is only the final assessment point of compulsory schooling. However, the processes of school mathematics education have been shown to work together in many intertwined ways to fulfil this function, for example, in national Key Stage tests and the use of these results in setting (see Chapter 2). Despite there being sufficient evidence to question the practice, there is a move to introduce more setting of children by 'ability' in UK schools. The arguments for this have become political, with the Conservative opposition party accusing the Labour government of reneging on its 1997 electoral commitment to increase setting in schools. The practice of ability grouping has been predominant in UK mathematics classrooms for many years. The arguments for continuing are apparently pragmatic but in reality are elitist; they are school selection in microcosm and damaging for many children and for the image of the subject.

Despite considerable political support, this is not the only obstacle for those wishing to challenge the dominance of this practice. If you are a relative newcomer to mathematics teaching, it is unlikely that you have seen how all-ability mathematics teaching can work. When, as a teacher educator, I talk with beginning teachers about alternative classroom practices and the evidence for their effectiveness, they are often unable to comprehend how such practice would work. For those that are open to the possibility of more equitable grouping practices and pedagogy there are ever-decreasing opportunities to see such practices. There is an urgent need for the dissemination of pedagogical approaches to mathematics teaching that can support all-ability teaching (Ollerton and Watson, 2005). Unfortunately, such priorities are not shared by the government or those advising them. Although the argument for such setting is based upon an apparent social justice argument, there is convincing evidence that good all-ability teaching might yield greater mathematical progress, interest and ongoing engagement, both within and beyond school (Boaler, 1997).

WHAT IS MATHEMATICS?

That there is a link between your personal beliefs (about education and mathematics) and the ways in which you will work as a teacher in the classrooms has already been mentioned. So, in order to consider the point of teaching mathematics in school we need to ask the question: 'What is mathematics?' The celebrated mathematics educator Hans Freudenthal (1991: 1), signals a note of caution when exploring this 'thorny question'. He warns that we 'don't look it up in the dictionary! Whenever I did the answer was wrong'. Despite the thorns, this question is important because the answer shapes what we think is important about mathematics, its place in the curriculum, the content of the curriculum and the pedagogies and resources that are used to develop it.

Much research in mathematics education has highlighted the relationship between teachers' espoused and enacted beliefs about mathematics and their classroom practice, which is important in the context of the discussion in this chapter. As Hersch (1986, cited in Thompson, 1992: 127) explains

> One's conception of what mathematics is affects one's conception of how it should be presented. One's manner of presenting it is an indication of what one believes to be most essential in it ... The issue, then, is not, What is the best way to teach? but, What is mathematics really all about?

Although Thompson is keen to point out that the relationship between beliefs and practices is not one of cause and effect, there is a sense elsewhere in this literature that beliefs help to generate teacher practice.

Discussions in the philosophy of mathematics education have explored whether mathematics is invented or discovered; whether it is absolute or fallible (Ernest, 1991; Lerman, 1990). Whilst you do not need to fully understand these arguments, it is important to recognize that your teacher beliefs are important and it is worth trying to understand why we do what we do. I have explored this with beginning teachers, with a particular interest in the metaphors that they use to describe mathematics and the process of learning mathematics (Noyes, 2006b). One of the predominant metaphors is that learning mathematics is a journey; this journey is linear and inspires competition; individuals can be located along this continuum and many of these beginning teachers signify their coming to like mathematics with being ahead of their peers:

> Mathematics is a journey, understanding one step leads to another, and each step relies on the existence of the previous one. This journey, for me, is what Mathematics is all about. It begins, at the beginning, with numbers and continues through (Brackets, Order, Division, Multiplication, Addition, Subtraction) BODMAS to calculus and statistics. How far each individual chooses to travel is up to him or her, but all must take the same initial steps. (Clara)

A second common metaphor is of mathematics as a language, even the pre-eminent language of nature (strong absolutist views are common): 'For me Mathematics is the poetry of the universe … To put Mathematics in context with other disciplines: Mathematics is the poetry of everything, or the language with which everything communicates with everything and how it relates to everything' (Steve). Thirdly, there is the utilitarian view that mathematics is a toolkit: 'It is perfectly reasonable to view mathematics as a toolkit, a bag of rules, methods and conventions that we can use to model, interpret or change the world around us' (Sarah).

It strikes me that these metaphors might lead to very different kinds of mathematical practices than if one considered doing mathematics to be an exploration (non-linear, messy), or the work of an artisan (who makes use of the tools to create mathematics). You might return at this point to the notes you made in response to the questions at the start of Part 1. Did you use any metaphors there, and to what extent do you think they indicate your beliefs about the teaching and learning of mathematics?

THE END OF A BEAUTIFUL ROMANCE?

This interest in metaphor relates to the theory of embodied cognition; that cognition is not simply about the brain but is mediated through physical experience. A recent thought-provoking view of the nature and origins of mathematics comes from this theoretical position. Lakoff and Nunez's (2000) *Where Mathematics Comes From* explains that mathematical cognition (and all understanding) develops from sensory experience. They argue that mathematics does not exist outside people – it is a human endeavour, a set of shifting social practices. A complex but persuasive argument leads them to raise some important points about the damaging impact of the traditional absolutist view of mathematics. This they call the 'romance of mathematics', a scientifically untenable position which maintains a mystique surrounding mathematicians and their practices.

> The Romance serves the purposes of the mathematical community. It helps to maintain an elite and then justify it. It is part of a culture that rewards incomprehensibility … The inaccessibility of most mathematical writings tends to perpetuate the romance and with it, its ill effects; the alienation of other educated people from mathematics, and the inaccessibility of mathematics to people who are interested in it and could benefit from it. Socially, the inaccessibility of mathematics has contributed to the lack of adequate mathematical training in the general populace in general. And that lack of adequate training contributes to an alarming trend – the division of our society into those who can function in an increasingly technical economy and those who cannot … it is contributing to the social and economic stratification of society. (Lakoff and Nunez, 2000: 341)

Whatever your conclusions about the nature of mathematics, and these recent developments in cognition theory are worth consideration, we need to recognize that mathematics as done by professional mathematicians is not necessarily the same as that experienced by children and teachers in school. The purposes and processes are generally quite different. We are not so concerned here with the question of what mathematics is, as this seems to be a philosophical concern, or how it is learned, which has been the preserve of the psychologist, although these are both important questions. What I am trying to focus your thinking on here is a more sociological and critical account of what mathematics does and allows us to do.

MATHEMATICS AND THE DIVINE

Mathematics is something that we have crafted for a variety of uses, rather than something which is absolute and transcendent. The sense of transcendence is not accidental as mathematics, the 'purest' of sciences, has often been ascribed as having divine origins (for example, by Newton). Lakoff and Nunez highlighted this to be a myth but the effect of this position is clear in what I have already written. However, there remains something sacrosanct about mathematics not only for those who argue for its link to future economic productivity (in industry, business and finance), but also for those defending its cultural status. Richard Winter thinks that the problem goes back to Pythagoras, and I include this lengthy quote as I so enjoy the richly religious overtones:

> the particular unfriendliness of mathematicians' ways of devaluing children's experience, however, is that in mathematics the power of the adult over the child is reinforced by the distant cultural echo of an ancient theological justification. At best the mathematics teacher approaches the child's experience as a benevolent theocratic despot. The difficult format of mathematical tasks ... confronts the child as divine wrath. The terror of the fifteen year old confronted by 'how many numbers are there between 0.41 and 0.42?' is the terror of the citizenry confronted by the pronouncements of the Delphic oracle, whose practical applications, wrapped in semantic mystery, were always only understood by the time it was 'too late'. And it is at least questionable whether most mathematics teachers, as priests of the mathematics temple, are unambiguously committed to liberating youthful citizens from their sense of awed subjection to its mystery. (Winter, 1992: 91)

Winter thinks the problems of mathophobia relate to how the supposed mystery and power of mathematics suppresses the playfulness that is necessary for learning. The emphasis on work rather than play stifles mathematical enjoyment so that doing mathematics in school is 'like being told to stop roller-skating and come in a tidy your room'. To what extent do you think this description relates to your own classroom?

Tom Popkewitz (2004: 251) echoes that same religious sense in which 'mathematics is one of the high priests of modernity' due to its lofty status in the enlightened age of social and intellectual progress. He also describes the process whereby mathematics as done in the academy is converted into a social practice that takes place in school as the 'alchemy of schooling'. The term 'mathematics' might be the same in describing what is done by mathematicians and what is part of the compulsory curriculum, but in fact they are two quite different things. They involve different social and cultural practices, have different political motivation and so on. This distinction that Popkewitz draws out is important here because we need to understand mathematics as the sets of practices in schools rather than mathematics as it is in academia.

Similarly, divine metaphors were used by my student teachers to denote the authority and power of mathematics (and to thereby assert its preeminence in a hierarchy of knowledge). This pantheistic elevation of mathematical language (for example, 'God is mathematics' [Ian]) mirrors Steve Lerman's (1990: 54) description of mathematics as 'the last bastion of absolutism'. For example:

- Mathematics is all around us. (Andy)
- Whether people like it or not mathematics is everywhere. (Alice)
- Most of the time we are not consciously performing mathematical operations, but we are still using (or being really) the mathematical nature of ourselves and the environment. (Steve)

But what are the roles of mathematics in schools and society? Here is one set of reasons, some of which have already been referred to:

> Let me begin by asking the question: to what end do we teach mathematics? Over the millenia, answers have been given and they have differed. Some of them have been: we teach it for its own sake, because it is beautiful; because it reveals the divine; because it helps us think logically; because it is the language of science and it helps us to understand and reveal the world; because it helps our students to get a job, either directly, in those areas of social or physical science that require mathematics, or directly, insofar as mathematics, through testing, acts as a social filter, admitting to certain professional possibilities those who can master the material. We teach it also to reproduce ourselves by producing future research mathematicians and mathematics teachers. (Davis, 1993: 190)

Where do your reasons fit into this list?

One of the difficulties that we have in exploring these questions of purpose is that such purposes are not common. Indeed, upon reading this quote you might easily identify with some of these ideas and be quite surprised by others. One strong argument put forward by scholars researching the social aspects of mathematics education is its formatting power. This formatting role is not fulfilled by mathematics per se but by users of mathematics – in this case teachers of *school mathematics* – and the ways it is organized and encountered by young people (Skovsmose, 1998). Its role as a gatekeeper has been well established in the UK for many years, regulating entrance to higher education and many courses in post-compulsory education.

> Mathematics is not only an impenetrable mystery to many, but has also, more than any other subject, been cast in the role as an 'objective' judge, in order to decide who in the society 'can' and 'cannot'. It therefore serves as *the* gate keeper to participation in the decision making processes of society. To deny some the access to participate in mathematics is then also to demonstrate, *a priori*, who will move ahead and who will stay behind. (Volmink, 1994: 51)

Not only is school mathematics different from mathematics as done in academia, but work of teachers is different. As a teacher, you would be hard pressed to deny that your work is political and very much embedded in the dominant ideologies, and social and cultural practices of the day. However, mathematics teachers need to recognize that the teaching of *school mathematics* is itself not culture-free or without social impact. In many ways the teacher's job is one of cultural production and reproduction. Once that argument is understood and accepted then you also need to consider whether the current products (for example, qualifications, attitudes, skills and so on) and modes of production (pedagogy, resources, and so on) are the most desirable and equitable.

REVISITING PURPOSE

I want to take some more time to consider a number of purposes for mathematics education as I think that this point is really important for you in understanding your own practice. The current curriculum privileges those who will proceed to A level and then use their mathematics in higher education, either directly in the mathematical sciences or through one of many applied routes in physical, life or social sciences. The curriculum has always been top-down and I will explore the history of this in more detail in Chapter 4. Here I pick up some aspects of the current model and begin to explore alternative rationale for mathematics curriculum design.

MATHEMATICS FOR THE ACADEMY

Academia and those professional mathematicians in science and industry have always been a dominant force in shaping the school curriculum. Much of the concern about the state of school mathematics surrounds the apparent poor quality of mathematical understanding of science, technology, engineering and mathematics (STEM) undergraduates; the poor supply of these graduates into science and industry; the downturn in A level uptake of mathematics courses and the alleged inadequacy of current compulsory school mathematics courses to prepare students for A level study. That these are serious issues is not in question, as the economy does require a supply of sufficiently skilled STEM graduates.

MATHEMATICS FOR EMPLOYMENT

Employability is a key policy driver for the improvement in school mathematics standards (Wolf, 2002). However, the nature of employment is changing and the global nature of economic markets is making for a different view of what it means to have a mathematically well-educated workforce in the twenty-first century. In the latter part of the twentieth century international comparisons of mathematical competence (Trends in International Mathematics and Science Study (TIMSS) and Programme for International Student Assessments (PISA)) contributed to a 'back-to-basics' neo-conservative trend in many parts of the world. Margaret Brown's (1998) analysis of 'the tyranny of the international horse race' highlighted the considerable methodological flaws in these kinds of international comparisons as well as the fact that they have probably had a more wide-ranging impact upon mathematics education than other subjects. If one retains that culture-neutral view of mathematics then such comparisons might be considered more objectively valuable, but hopefully at this point you would agree that school mathematics is somehow dialectically related to the cultural and social context in which it is taught. Such an international stage opens up the way for the more powerful players to determine what is important mathematical knowledge for the twenty-first century. This is all highly politicized and although some interesting comparisons of the national differences have been made (for example, Stigler and Hiebert, 1999) there is still the need to critique these discourses of globalization.

Although the global knowledge economy is clearly important as we anticipate more international migration of workers and work, local knowledge is equally, if not more, important. As business and industry become more specialized so, too, do the mathematical practices integrated into those workspaces. Moreover, ubiquitous technological support is changing the types of mathematics practices yet further. So the political argument for a mathematically competent workforce is grounded in a utilitarianism that supports a curriculum that is perhaps inappropriate for the increasingly diverse knowledges required in modern society. In contrast the school mathematics curriculum has changed little in structure, content and delivery. Admittedly there have been attempts to reinvigorate curriculum and pedagogy in the last 20 years, but this has arguably had limited impact (consider, for example, Brown et al.'s [2003] analysis of the National Numeracy Strategy). In some cases the impact has been quite the reverse. For example, the report by Adrian Smith (2004) describes the 'disastrous' impact of the Curriculum 2000 reforms upon participation in post-compulsory mathematics study.

Whilst academia's demands and those of the employers have so far been about the well-qualified graduate, there has been a parallel concern about the basic skills of the UK workforce. Bynner and Parsons (1997) highlighted the relationship between poor levels of numeracy and unemployability, and that this correlation was in fact stronger than between poor levels of adult literacy and employability. Apparently in order for these people to contribute to economic productivity their mathematical skills need to be improved. Two years later, official reports painted a bleak picture of poor numeracy skills amongst the UK's adult population. The Labour government proceeded to spend huge sums of money on rectifying this problem. That this initiative has been strongly criticized is perhaps unsurprising. To imagine that after 11 years of compulsory schooling those who left school with little or no mathematics qualification could be upskilled so easily is naive.

What has happened in recent years is the increased momentum of the skills agenda, and this was at the heart of the Tomlinson recommendations on the future of the 14–19 curriculum (DfES, 2004). Hence the notion of numeracy has morphed into something called 'functional mathematics'. If numeracy was a slippery term, then this notion of functionality, rooted in the utilitarian metaphor of mathematics being a set of tools for work and life, is perhaps even more so. What function does this mathematics perform? The double meaning highlights again that not only is mathematics useful to one who has it, but that school mathematics does things to people; it functions in society. Trials of these functional mathematics courses are beginning as

I write, but we are still not clear about what functional mathematics really is. As you will have seen from what you have read so far, there are many functions and having one so named course is really nonsensical. Moreover, the situatedness of mathematical practices (that is, their particular relevance for the context in which they are learned and practiced) and the powerful influence of assessment on curriculum raises questions regarding whether or not *functional mathematics* will achieve much – time will tell.

So are school mathematics classrooms simply production lines? Are schools just training employees of the future? Although this might be the unspoken yet agreed purpose of the curriculum as it stands, it is my belief that school mathematics should be more deliberate in its aim to prepare citizens for active participation in democratic society. So whereas school mathematics is clearly important to future employees and academia it should have other equally important priorities. A broadening of curricular and pedagogic purpose is key to reinvigorating interest and engagement in the learning of mathematics.

MATHEMATICS FOR GENERAL EDUCATION

Hans Werner Heymann's (2003) thorough exploration of the question 'why teach mathematics?' make a strong case that it be part of a general education. He explains that:

> A great number of children, adolescents, and adults encounter enormous difficulties with mathematics. For these people, the difficulties are intrinsic in the distinctive characteristics of the subject matter. In many cases, the mathematics which they are obliged to learn in schools only attains the status of knowledge required for examinations – learned superficially and, correspondingly, quickly forgotten again. (Heymann, 2003: 1)

Although his context is the German education system, many teachers would share his view that if everything beyond the first seven years of compulsory schooling were to be forgotten there would not be much damage done to one's prospects in life. So where does that leave you if you are a secondary mathematics teacher? He goes on to assert that 'conventional mathematics instruction in schools does justice neither to foreseeable societal demands nor to the individual needs and qualification interests of a majority of adolescents' (Heymann, 2003: 2). Heymann is critical of the way in which mathematics educators can become so focused on the detail of their own discipline that they fail to take account of the larger educational and social context in which mathematics teaching is situated.

While Heymann retains the notion of *preparation for later life*, understood more broadly than just employability, he also suggests that the *promotion of cultural competence* should be a core theme of mathematics education based upon a model of general education. Thirdly, mathematics is used to *develop an understanding of the world* that goes beyond 'fabricated' contexts seen in so many classrooms and texts. Fourthly, and more focused on classroom pedagogy, he suggests that mathematics should promote *understanding, cognitive skills and critical thinking*, although I think that use of the word 'critical' is not the same as that discussed below. Finally his list of five core themes moves on to consider the classroom environment and the impact that this has upon the learner. He envisages a classroom in which the *willingness to assume responsibility, communication and co-operation, enhances the students' self-esteem*. He points out that none of these elements are new but that together they might offer something of a new profile for mathematics education. Aspects of this profile have been referred to already and others will be picked up below. The notion of cultural competence is a theme of the UK National Curriculum but rarely gets taken up by mathematics teachers.

MATHEMATICS FOR CITIZENSHIP

Whereas we are not, in the UK, used to talking about general education, other than in contrasting primary school generalism and secondary level specialism, we do have a loosely related notion of citizenship. In reality the idea of citizenship education is a contested one. In the UK in recent years there has been concern about political engagement and following the Crick report (QCA, 1998) recommendations were made regarding the inclusion of citizenship education in schools. In the last few years, schools have had a mandatory obligation to 'deliver' citizenship using the newly designed National Curriculum for Citizenship. Schools generally adopted one of a number of implementation models, either embedding the work across the curriculum or, more commonly, as a stand-alone taught curriculum. In some schools citizenship is now the C in PSCHE, what was personal, social and health education. Having already highlighted the tendency of mathematics teachers to deny the value-laden nature of school mathematics, it is perhaps unsurprising that most mathematics teachers did not see education for citizenship (as constituted in this curriculum) as their domain.

This form of citizenship education is not what I am describing here. Hilary Povey (2003) has offered a critique of this policy from a mathematics educator perspective. She argues that education for citizenship is closely related to education for social justice and that as such classroom mathematics needs to be more reflexive. In this way we can begin to see how mathematics is used by, and on, various members of society and in classrooms. She makes the important point that 'to harness mathematics learning for social justice involves rethinking and reframing mathematics classrooms so that both the relationship between participants and the relationship of participants to mathematics (as well as the mathematics itself) is changed' (Povey, 2003: 56). So, although I have been arguing for a rethinking of the curriculum, Povey reminds us that this cannot happen without a reconceptualization of the relationships and practices of mathematics classrooms. A classroom where mathematics and citizenship education run in parallel is developing a more socially just ethos through its practices as well as in the content and delivery of the curriculum. You might like to look at the classrooms in which you are working and ask yourself whether or not the experiences of learners are founded upon principles of social justice.

CRITICAL MATHEMATICS EDUCATION

The concept and practice of critical mathematics education (Skovsmose, 1994) has much in common with education for citizenship. There is an explicit aim to make one of the foci of classroom mathematics activity the critique of societal power relationships. In these classrooms mathematics is used to make sense of the social and scientific dimensions of the world in ways that uncover the value-laden nature of mathematics.

It has been suggested that the lack of mathematics graduates may have a negative impact on future economic prosperity. Though we cannot deny the importance of mathematics in the fabric of modern society, we must be clear about the fact that social advancement is not simply about economic growth. Moreover, the economy and the mathematical knowledge utilized within does not always lead to better life circumstances for the members of that society or other societies. Through various applications of mathematics (science, technology and engineering) we have improved transport, the design of life-saving drugs and email privacy. On the other hand, there is a global arms trade, nuclear weapons, digital fraud, and so on. A critical mathematics curriculum uses mathematics to ask hard questions about social injustice on both a local and global level. More than that, such a curriculum should lead to not only better understanding of the world in which we live, but individual and collective action that is aimed at challenging and transforming the world for the better, what Eric Gutstein (2006) calls 'writing the world with mathematics'.

MATHEMATICS FOR THE INFORMATION AGE

This brief introduction to some of the main purposes for mathematics education has moved from the well-documented and current, taken-for-granted employability and skills rationale to the more problematic (for a neo-conservative administration) rationale of critical thinking. Before moving on it is worth considering briefly the issue of the future of the mathematics curriculum. We are in a period of sustained and considerable change in the UK education system in which Every Child Matters legislation (DfES, 2003) and the move to greater school autonomy suggests that further change might be just around the corner.

What does all this mean for mathematics in the knowledge or information society and for you as teachers of mathematics for the near – and possibly distant – future? What kinds of mathematical knowledge skills and understanding will be desirable in 10 or 20 years' time? How will increasingly powerful computer applications impact upon schools, learning and, in particular, mathematics? Mike Newby (2005: 298–9), working on the DfES Teaching 2020 project, has intimated some possible future scenarios:

> The *subject content* (such as it is taught in schools, for it will be available everywhere) will be in a constant state of flux, barriers between disciplines crumbling, established subjects coming to blend and morph into new ones ...
>
> The *contingent* nature of knowledge will therefore require learners in the schools of the future to acquire qualities of thought and action which will suit them to succeed in a world with fewer certainties and greater risks

Meanwhile the Chief Advisor for Mathematics, Celia Hoyles, and her colleagues have pointed out that 'mathematics education in the third millennium will not just be about teaching and learning mathematics, but about the nature of knowledge and the place of mathematics within society' (Hoyles et al., 1999: 3). I will return to these ideas in the final chapter of the book when looking ahead to possible future curriculum directions.

SUMMARY

So what is the point of doing mathematics in school? If the concern of academia is for the future supply of mathematics and mathematics-related graduates and their preparation then this only concerns a minority of the school population. If the aim is workforce employability, then are schoolchildren in mathematics classrooms on a production line in which skills, numeracy and functionality are all-important? On the other hand, if education is concerned for the whole person then these two positions are insufficient.

We know that under the current regime many learners are not engaged with learning mathematics and decide to cease studying it at the earliest possible opportunity. As a teacher of mathematics, if you are genuinely concerned about the education and future well-being of young people then the notion of a general education needs to be central. The problem is that the current curriculum is not predicated upon a model of general education, and that is not how pupils are assessed or how your effectiveness is measured. If general education as experienced in the mathematics classroom is not simply about academic knowledge but about practical knowledge and action, then a case for more citizenship education and even critical education in mathematics classrooms can be made. The question then is what must change in order to introduce, or give greater prominence to, these generalist themes? Heymann offers some reassurance when he suggests that 'the path to instruction oriented more strongly toward general education cannot be enforced from external sources ... but can only consist of small steps involving many participants for whom these steps make good sense' (Heymann, 2003: 8). No doubt the same could be said of a mathematics curriculum oriented toward critical citizenship.

Paul Ernest's (1992) analysis of the origins of the Mathematics NC showed a similar set of influences. He explained how the 'old humanists' (those in academia) and 'industrial trainers' (the employers) dominated the new curriculum, marginalizing the child-centred 'progressive educators'. One group – the 'public educators' – were not given any say whatsoever. These public educators

> represent a radical reforming tradition, concerned with democracy and social equity ... to empower the working classes to participate in the democratic institutions of society, and to share more fully in the prosperity of modern industrial society ...
> ... represent radical reformers who see mathematics as a means to empower students: mathematics is to give them the confidence to pose problems, initiate investigations and autonomous projects; to critically examine and question the use of mathematics and statistics in our increasingly mathematized society, combating the mathematical mystification prevalent in the treatment of social and political issues. (Ernest, 1992: 36)

These are the critical educators; teachers who are interested in a more radical citizenship education and education for social justice in the mathematics classroom. Ernest's work describes the power struggle for influence and it is ironic that the only group that emphazises the need to expose the nature of power through the mathematics curriculum is the group that was relatively powerless in shaping the new curriculum. This influence, along with that of the progressive educators, needs to be reintroduced to the curriculum.

Further questions to consider

What are your own intentions/aims when teaching mathematics?

Which elements of Davis's list are you most/least in agreement with? Would you add anything? How might these various purposes shape classroom mathematics practices?

Teaching (mathematics) is, by nature of the fact it is a core component of the national education system, a political activity! How does your own personal politics influence your thinking about the purposes of teaching mathematics?

Department for Education and Skills (DfES) (2004) *14–19 Reform Final Report*. London: Department for Education and Skills.
Department for Education and Skills (DfES) (2005) *14–19 Education and Skills*. London: HMSO.

Together with the Smith report, the Tomlinson report of 14–19 education and skills and the subsequent government White Paper will be highly influential in mathematics teaching over the next few years.

Smith, A. (2004) *Making Mathematics Count*. London: The Stationery Office.

Every teacher will have heard of the Smith report but it is worth reading as the implications for teachers of mathematics are considerable. It is available, or can be purchased, online. Even a read of the executive summary would be informative.

THE MATHEMATICS CURRICULUM

Education systems evolve along with the societies in which they are situated, and so the mathematics curriculum also evolves. In this chapter we will consider one historical account of the mathematics curriculum in England and in so doing we will try to understand how we have got to the point at which we now find ourselves. Having established that there are various groups with different purposes for school mathematics you will now try to account for how these interests have shaped the curriculum as it is experienced today. This is important for any teacher so that they can understand how their own classroom practice is and has been shaped. In recognizing these constraining influences we can then consider the possibilities for change as well as acknowledge the challenges facing teachers who want to teach mathematics in a different way.

CHANGE IS HERE TO STAY!

So far in this book we have considered some general problems of mathematics education, types of mathematics learning and patterns of choice and attainment, and have begun to explore different purposes for mathematics education. These various factors are interrelated with one another and with the focus of this chapter – the curriculum. The curriculum of today has evolved in recent decades, at some times quite suddenly and with significant consequences. Between the time I completed my school mathematics and when I started teaching, a National Curriculum had been introduced. If you are reading this book as a new teacher of mathematics you might well have only ever learnt mathematics under one form or another of the National Curriculum. Alongside that you might not be able to conceive of a school system without Ofsted, league tables or a national Framework for Teaching Mathematics. And the generation is passing that remember the new mathematics of the 1960s and even perhaps the Cockcroft report of 1982. I have heard senior colleagues in schools and academia echoing the sentiment that 'what goes around comes around' in mathematics education but perhaps it is more helpful to use Mark Twain's saying that 'history does not repeat itself, but it does rhyme'. This chapter offers one brief telling of the complex rhymes of mathematics curriculum history.

This steady evolution of the purposes, content and pedagogy of the curriculum is framed by the political and educational priorities of the day, themselves shifting and sometimes unpredictable. Despite this unpredictability there are trends in mathematics education that are reflections of wider social change, particularly in the internationalized culture of the information, or *informational*, age. This strong linkage might suggest that offering an alternative trajectory for the future direction of mathematics in school would be a futile exercise. Developing such an alternative requires an understanding of the trajectory of the recent mathematics curriculum. It would be all too easy to suggest alternatives which are disconnected to the current realities of mathematics classrooms.

It is important to remember that curriculum can be understood at various levels. There is the mandated curriculum that can be traced through official policy and other texts, but this does not necessarily equate to the curriculum organized in school or that experienced by learners in a particular mathematics group.

One of the reasons for exploring the history of the official, espoused curriculum is to trace today's discourses of mathematics education and terms such as 'numeracy', 'mathemacy' and 'functional mathematics'. This will enable us to consider the current policies that are shaping the development of school mathematics teaching. The evolution of the mathematics curriculum has not happened in isolation from, for example, the move to comprehensive schooling in the middle of the twentieth century or the introduction of GCSEs in the late 1980s, so I will begin by retracing the development of the modern-day school and the place of mathematics within it.

MATHEMATICS FOR ALL

Manual Castells (2000) describes how we are currently undergoing an 'informational revolution', in a similar way to which earlier agricultural and industrial developments marked drastic revolutionary moments in the development of societies. In the 'informational society' it is the production, management and distribution of information that is the core driver of the economy and the prime source of power – Francis Bacon's well-known dictum 'knowledge is power' was several centuries ahead of its time. I want to commence this brief history of mathematics curriculum with the arrival of the industrial revolution that transformed the Western world through the eighteenth and nineteenth centuries and leading up to the start of the twentieth century.

Leo Rogers (1998) explains how, as part of the Industrial Revolution, the 100 years from 1750 to 1850 saw a dramatic expansion in the need for practical applications and knowledge of science and mathematics. Universities that had for so long been the custodians of mathematics education for the elite few were gradually accompanied by other organizations and institutions offering the more open public education, often focused on science and mathematics, required in the new industrial society. These applications were not so concerned with the mathematics of the ancients but the more utilitarian and experimental applications of mathematics demanded by industry. So it was that the emerging demand for mathematics learning helped to engrain a class division that remains endemic to mathematics education: mathematics for the workers or mathematics for the 'well educated'. By the early part of the nineteenth century radical working-class leaders were beginning to demand education for all; a demand which was considered politically dangerous and initially was opposed.

The English public school system (which was really not public at all) of the nineteenth century initially had little mathematics in its liberal curriculum. Rogers describes that elsewhere, non-conformist and military schools also developed in the middle part of that century, the latter with a far more contemporary curriculum (and an interest in warfare, of course). These opportunities to be schooled and learn mathematics were not open to women, although change was afoot. Throughout this formative stage of the development of the school curriculum something important was happening which is still in effect today. The liberal curriculum of the universities remained in place in the public schools that supplied them. Meanwhile the range of applications of science was expanding and mathematics was being developed in the various experimental/practical contexts of this new industrial world. The roots of our modern school mathematics curriculum are in the class system of the Victorian era. The public school/university liberal mathematics curriculum was already divided from the utilitarian workplace mathematics applications.

MATHEMATICS IN THE 3 Rs

By the 1870s the demand for universal education had been partially realized and England had been subdivided into over 2,000 school districts. In each of these an elected school board oversaw the provision of elementary education for the working-class children. These schools catered for children up to the age of 14 and focused on the 3 Rs; reading, writing and arithmetic. The Conservative government of 1902 scrapped the school boards, despite opposition from the Labour Party and established local education authorities (LEAs) with the power to set up new secondary and technical schools. It was at this time that the modern subject-oriented curriculum emerged. The controversy surrounding this Education act continued and the Conservatives lost the next election.

Four decades later the 1944 Education Act set out to establish the foundations of the post-war education system. All children would take an 11+ examination and would subsequently attend one of three tiers of school – grammar, secondary modern or technical – up to the compulsory leaving age of 15. Grammar schools had been in existence for hundreds of years, some having become fee-paying in the nineteenth century. However, restricted access was now politically mandated and, in response, some LEAs resisted this process of selection and tiered schooling and instead experimented with comprehensive schools. Although at first there was political opposition to this radical idea of comprehensive schooling, by the 1960s the Labour Party of the day was in support of a general move to comprehensive schooling and, when it formed a new government in 1964, instructed local authorities to move towards comprehensive schooling.

Notably absent in this account of school development is the (mathematics) curriculum but what is clear is the process whereby societal hierarchies that existed before the Industrial Revolution were then legitimated by the different education demands of the workers and the elite. Up until the 1980s and the introduction of the National Curriculum for England and Wales, schools had considerable autonomy over curriculum content. This is not to say that there was no politics of curriculum, for as we have seen from the Industrial Revolution there has been a separation between liberal and utilitarian principles for mathematics curriculum design. Johnston Anderson (2002) provides some snapshots of mathematics education from the time when compulsory schooling was introduced in the 1870s through until the 1970s. He shows that much of the contemporary debates about curriculum, pedagogy and assessment *rhyme* with concerns stretching back 130 years. Even in 1876, elementary schools were certified 'efficient' if half their pupils passed two of the three tests covering the three Rs; with half of those having passed in arithmetic. Despite having a contemporary curriculum containing many subjects, it is still these 'core' subjects that are the critical measure of a school's success, even more so now as those reported as having attained five or more GCSE A*–C passes must include English and mathematics.

MODERN MATHEMATICS

Through the second half of the twentieth century there was a growing political assumption that economic productivity and successful international trading were linked to the quality and quantity of school education (Wolf, 2002). The scene was set for the introduction of the NC for England and Wales in 1988 which ushered in a new era for UK schools. This followed on the heels of broader developments and discussions that had been taking place in school mathematics throughout the previous 25 years. One such initiative in this *modern* mathematics was the School Mathematics Project (SMP), supposedly designed for those who would finish their mathematical study upon completion of compulsory school, but which would also be suitable for those continuing to A level and beyond. Anderson (2002: 12) lists some of the aims of that original SMP programme:

- To make school mathematics more exciting and enjoyable
- To impart a knowledge of the nature of mathematics and its uses in the modern world
- To encourage more pupils to pursue further the study of mathematics

- To bridge the gulf between university and school mathematics (in both content and outlook)
- To reflect the changes brought about by increased automation and the introduction of computers.

These are laudable aims covering three broader themes.

1   There is the concern to increase engagement by making lessons 'exciting and enjoyable'; many aspiring teachers interviewed for teacher education courses describe much of their own learning of mathematics in school as being far from exciting. One of the most common ideas for mathematics education amongst new teachers is that lessons should be more fun, but whether more fun will increase engagement remains to be seen (although there is some evidence to support this). This aim risks sidestepping the questions about curricular aims and content.

2   There are two types of utilitarianism; that children need to know how mathematics is used in the modern world, and that they should understand this particularly in the context of new information technology (IT) applications.

3   There is the concern for the mathematician of the future. This does not mean that the second and third aims are independent but could represent the two strands of mathematics that have their roots in the Industrial Revolution.

Despite the progress made through projects like SMP, school mathematics remained an object of criticism in this pre-NC era. As the NC was being introduced, Alan Bishop (1988) summarized four main criticisms of mathematics teaching at that time. He concluded that a 'technique-oriented curriculum', through which learners memorize routines that could be more easily carried out by a computer, 'cannot help understanding, cannot develop meaning, cannot enable the learner to develop a critical stance either inside or outside mathematics' (Bishop, 1988: 7). Such a curriculum is predicated upon the mistaken notion that mathematics is value-free and so does not value personal and local knowledge but rather privileges 'impersonal learning'. This process of depersonalization is, he asserts, 'non educational' (Bishop, 1988: 10). The impersonal process is supported by an overreliance on textbook schemes. This argument has been explored by other commentators such as Michael Apple (1993), who has written about the politics of the textbook, explaining that the realized curricula of schools is as much a product of market-driven textbook schemes as it is of any national curriculum.

Around the same time that the NC was launched, an international group of scholars published their scenarios for *School Mathematics in the 1990s* (Howson and Wilson, 1986). This explored the possible shifting aims and curriculum content of mathematics education both within a general education and in a technological society. 'It seems self-evident that the Information Revolution will result in major changes in both schools and their curricula, as new demands are made and new opportunities provided for teaching and learning in educational systems across the world' (Howson and Wilson, 1986: 2).

Has this happened? How much more change is coming and what impact has this really had upon mathematics learning? As it happens the group's forward-looking scenarios have been overtaken by the educational politics of the last 20 years. Despite the government's support for the increased use of technology this is yet to filter through to significantly improved classroom learning. The international approach of Howson and Wilson's book is interesting but raises the question of whether or not it is desirable for mathematics education to be internationalized. What the group did propose, following the same line as Bishop, is two alternative approaches to the place of values in mathematics teaching:

- Alternative 1: Mathematics is neutral, and is best taught in isolation from contentious social issues.
- Alternative 2: Since mathematics underpins both technology in all its manifold forms, and the policies that determine how it is used, its teaching should deliberately be related to these issues.

They lead the reader towards alternative 2, which of course I applaud. They also made other interesting proposals that would be worth considering.

THE COCKCROFT REPORT

In those pre-NC years between the development of new syllabi and the work of Bishop and others, a major report on mathematics education was published (Cockcroft, 1982). In response to ongoing criticism of school mathematics the Committee of Inquiry into the Teaching of Mathematics in Schools was commissioned. The terms of reference for the committee were: 'To consider the teaching of mathematics in primary and secondary schools in England and Wales, with particular regard to the mathematics required in further and higher education, employment and adult life generally, and to make recommendations' (Cockcroft, 1982: ix). The report offered 'constructive and original proposals for change' and although it was a landmark report it seems from what followed that the impact was not all that had been hoped for. Nevertheless, for many, the report provided some inspiration for the development of a more diverse classroom culture where discussion and investigational approaches were privileged, as evidenced in the oft quoted paragraph 243 (Cockcroft, 1982: 71):

mathematics teaching at all levels should include opportunities for
- exposition by the teacher
- discussion between teacher and pupils and between pupils themselves
- appropriate practical work
- consolidation and practice of fundamental skills and routines
- problem solving, including the application of mathematics to everyday situations
- investigational work.

Laurinda Brown and Jo Waddingham's 'addendum to Cockcroft' (1982) provided teachers with a collection of ideas to use in their lessons. The interest in investigational mathematics was later to become embedded in the new NC but, without a genuine shift in teacher beliefs about the purpose of this kind of mathematics learning, this has been another aspect of classroom mathematics that has not been fully transformed in the ways hoped for at the time.

THE NATIONAL CURRICULUM

In 1988 the National Curriculum for England and Wales was introduced with 10 foundation subjects. The rationale for this selection was not given (White, 2004: 2) but there was notable similarity with the range of subjects introduced in 1904. So this new NC was not built upon a set of underpinning aims or principles, although it did have two broad aims, described by White as 'platitudinous'. Over time these two aims have become:

- The school curriculum should aim to provide opportunities for all pupils to learn and to achieve.
- The school curriculum should aim to promote pupils' spiritual, moral, social and cultural development and prepare all pupils for the opportunities, responsibilities and experiences of adult life.

The mathematics curriculum does very little to meet this second aim. At the time of its introduction there was understandably plenty of available critique of a centralized curriculum (for example, Dowling and Noss, 1990) but now, nearly 20 years on, the NC has become taken for granted. The original NC for mathematics was fragmented into 14 attainment targets each with 10 levels. The complexity has been reduced with successive iterations of the curriculum but many of the original problems remain. One of these is the notion that levels actually mean something and a worrying trend in recent years has been the statistically nonsensical use of part levels (for example, Jimmy is level 5.2). Whereas the original national tests of children's progress on this curriculum made some attempt to identify questions with levels, this has gone, to be replaced by numerical marks and level boundaries. However, whatever means you use to construct such levelled-ness it remains an arbitrary fabrication and at base a ranking system.

OLD AND NEW CURRICULAR GEOMETRY

One interesting view of this debate about levels comes from Brent Davis and Dennis Sumara (2000). They argue that models of curriculum have always been of a Euclidian form, with a mistaken belief that you can break it down to smaller and smaller units which get simpler and together comprise the whole. This is what we see in schools today with a fragmented curriculum and learning process; each lesson has stated objectives (as if that means that learning will take place), medium- and long-term plans serve to atomize the learning process in unnatural and unhelpful ways. Davis and Sumara (2000: 828) suggest that curriculum would be better understood as fractal where 'the part is not simply a fragment of the whole, it is a fractal out of which the whole unfolds and in which the whole is enfolded'. That certainly seems to fit my experiences of teaching and learning mathematics and might well resonate with you.

Using complexity theory to understand the development of mathematical knowledge, skills and understanding means that we need to take on board the findings of Jo Boaler's study (1997), in which the tightly regimented, structured mathematics curriculum in one of two broadly equivalent schools had a relatively detrimental effect on the learners. Of course, adopting such different approaches might mean changing your beliefs (if that is possible) or at the very least being in a position to consider the alternatives. What you do need to do is get underneath the language of the NC with its levels and pro-grammes, and ask whether all this structure helps the learning process or in some ways hinders it. The important point here is that we need to critique this taken-for-granted curriculum, recognizing how it has been shaped by various political purposes.

A NATIONAL STRATEGY FOR NUMERACY

Having documented the development of a mathematics curriculum and the ever-present criticism of mathematics education it comes as no surprise that the NC, with its promise of better curriculum continuity, was not a cure-all. While the NC prescribed the curriculum, it did not transform classroom pedagogy or attitudes to learning mathematics. During the 1990s a strategy for raising attainment in mathematics was devised and 'rolled out'; the National Numeracy Strategy was first introduced to primary schools and then into secondary classrooms at the turn of the millenium.

But just what was this new numeracy? Many terms in everyday use have a wide range of meanings, and numeracy is no exception. The Crowther report of 1959 gave an introductory definition of numeracy as 'An under-standing of the scientific approach to the study of phenomena – observation, hypothesis, experiment, verification ... the need in the modern world to think quantitatively, to realise how far our problems are problems of degree even when they appear as problems of kind' (p. 270, cited in Noss, 2002: 33). From a review of submissions to the Cockcroft committee some years later the conclusion was made that 'the words [numeracy/numerate] have changed their meaning considerably in the last twenty years' to denote little more than an ability to 'perform basic arithmetical operations' (DES, 1982: 11). The committee expressed the view that being numerate should mean the possession of two attributes:

The first of these is an 'at-homeness' with numbers and an ability to make use of mathematical skills which enables an individual to cope with the practical mathematical demands of everyday life. The second is an ability to have some appreciation and understanding of information which is presented in mathematical terms, for instance in graphs, charts or tables or by reference to percentage increase or decrease. (Cockcroft, 1982: 11)

The first attribute returns us to the idea of utility, whereby mathematics is useful in life. This dimension of Cockcroft's numeracy is now at the heart of the functional mathematics that was introduced by the Tomlinson report on 14–19 education, adopted in the skills White Paper (DfES, 2005) and now appearing in schools. The second attribute of being numerate seems particularly relevant in an era where information bombards us daily and we are called upon to make some critical sense of this.

THE DEMISE OF DATA HANDLING?

The privileged position of data handling in the curriculum, particularly in the 14–19 phase, is at risk. The Smith report (Smith, 2004: 7) recommended a radical rethink of the location of statistics and data handling: '[it would] be better removed from the mathematics timetable and integrated with the teaching and learning of other disciplines (e.g. biology or geography). The time restored to the mathematics timetable should be used for acquiring greater mastery of core mathematical concepts and operations.' This would be very concerning for a number of reasons. First, the agenda here is that of higher education and in particular physical and engineering science, rather than on what might be beneficial in a general education. Secondly, the kinds of data-awareness necessary might not be best served in these classrooms. A geographer colleague explained how GCSE students were rewarded for the widest range of chart types in their coursework rather than whether they were most appropriate for the purpose. Several of my past A level students ended up teaching statistical components of their social science courses when the teacher was not comfortable with discussing, for example, normal distributions. Thirdly, this move would serve to maintain the abstracted, value-free notion of mathematics that we questioned earlier.

Let us return to the idea of numeracy. At first numeracy seemed to become a substitute for mathematics, at least in the primary school (my daughters at primary school still talk about what they did in numeracy – much to my irritation). By the time the strategy reached secondary school it had become the Framework for Teaching Mathematics but although the title had changed the underlying principles were very much the same. The Framework was not mandatory but was often accepted as such. Secondary-level mathematics teacher trainees are still given a free copy (but had to buy their own NC) and the language of the strategy (now part of the National Strategy for Key Stage 3 and beyond) has become normal. In a majority of schools teachers will talk about the three-part lesson as if this is the only way to teach. This formulaic approach has been adopted with little critique from teachers. Does learning really happen in convenient chunks of 1 hour divided into three sections?

One representative of the National Strategy was talking to our beginning teachers and raised my hopes that the nonsense of the three-part lesson would be ended: 'a lesson does not necessarily need three parts', she said 'but it should have a beginning, a middle and an end'! This amused me but it passed by most of the audience.

Is learning really like a book with a beginning, a middle and an end? My learning is rarely like that but is, rather, diffuse and unpredictable, with surprises and disappointments, undefined beginnings and unfinished chapters. This kind of messy learning requires a far more flexible, contingent approach to teaching, which does not fit well into our timetable or with the current school inspection regime.

KEY SKILLS AND FUNCTIONAL MATHEMATICS

The Labour government since 1997 has not only overseen the continuation of numeracy initiative begun by the Conservatives but has also developed a strong basic skills agenda. Around the same time as Curriculum 2000 was being introduced with its new structure for A level study, Key Skills were high on the agenda. Application of Number could be accredited at various levels and it was expected that along with Communication and ICT students would apply for university places with these 'skill' qualifications complementing their traditional A level qualifications. It soon became clear that not all universities would take these into account, and they quickly became unimportant and superfluous to requirements for most students. However, while the Key Skills qualifications faded, the new AS and A2 mathematics qualifications had a rather more dramatic effect, with disproportionately high numbers of students failing their AS exams at the end of Year 12 and then opting not to continue, the problem with A level recruitment was exacerbated.

Mathematical pathways from 14–19 are being reviewed in light of the Tomlinson and Smith reports, and both of these areas will be reinvigorated. Not only is there now a two-tiered GCSE system that will allow all pupils to sit an examination on which it is possible to gain a grade C, but in order to get that grade they will have to demonstrate their ability in the aforementioned *functional mathematics*. 'Achieving functional skills in English and mathematics must be at the heart of the 14–19 phase. These skills are essential to support learning in other subjects and they are essential for employment. Achieving level 2 (GCSE level) in functional English and mathematics is a vital part of a good education' (DfES, 2005: 6).

SUMMARY

In this chapter we have considered various dimensions of the school mathematics curriculum and its evolution over several generations. One of the points made in the recent inquiry into post-14 mathematics education (Smith, 2004: 6) highlights the need for curricula rethink when it explains that 'the overwhelming majority of respondents to the inquiry no longer regard current mathematics curricula, assessment and qualifications as fit for purpose'. We might ask 'What purpose', or perhaps more importantly 'Whose purposes'?

Throughout the history of the curriculum there has remained the division between what I described earlier as the liberal curriculum and the applied curriculum. In the Industrial Revolution this curricular bifurcation divided people's experience of mathematics depending upon their social status, and in some ways the same is true today. The distinction between mathematics and numeracy, or mathematics and functional mathematics, hints at the continuation of two streams of mathematics (although the situation is far more complex in reality). Even Smith's separation of 'core mathematical concepts' and 'statistics and data handling' has the same underlying spirit but now data is the everyday medium of the information age and the core mathematical concepts are those demanded by 'many in higher education'.

The curriculum and its various strands have and always will be highly political, and teachers need to understand what this means for them and for the learners in their classes. Moreover, the curriculum's props (for example, the assessment regime or print and digital resources) are having an increasing influence over curriculum and pedagogy. However, whereas this was once controlled by the bigger educational publishers and examination boards, there is now the fragmentation of online sources which are creeping into many mathematics classrooms. Through all of this there is a need to stand back and ask again whose interests are being served and if, as Smith reports, the current curricula are not fit for purpose, then what should and could be in their place?

Questions for reflection

Which strands of curriculum tradition can you recognize in your own experience and in the classrooms to which you now have access?

In your experience of teaching mathematics, to what extent and how has the second aim of the National Curriculum been addressed?

Peter Gill concluded that there was the need for a radical rethink of the curriculum. For which learners and in what ways do you consider the NC to be 'fit (or unfit) for purpose'?

What is your position on the removal of data handling from the mathematics curriculum?

REBALANCING THE CURRICULUM

So far we have been considering the case for a radical rethink of mathematics education and the curriculum that frames the experiences of children in schools. That is not to say that all is not good, but rather there is an imbalance in the curriculum that tends to favour certain groups of learners. Moreover, the politics and history of mathematics education is moving in a certain direction which is not good for all young people.'

This chapter is a shorter, transitionary one in which you will begin to consider how mathematics education might be redirected in the hope of challenging mathophobia and disengagement. We begin with a set of principles that might be helpful guides in this rethink and relate them to the general aims of the NC, the development of critical citizenship and the mobilization of *public educators*.

CONSIDERING THE ALTERNATIVES

Having established that there are significant challenges facing mathematics educators and learners at the beginning of the twenty-first century, let us begin to consider possible alternatives in more detail. What directions might teachers, curriculum developers and policy-makers explore if there is to be a significant shift of attitudes to the learning of mathematics, and to increasing post-compulsory engagement with the subject? Peter Gates, in the introduction to *Issues in Mathematics Teaching* says that 'hating mathematics is as much a national pastime as complaining about the weather and mathophobia is so acceptable ... it is a very serious matter' (Gates, 2001: 7).

Questions to consider before reading this chapter

Having read the preceding chapters, what might you do to improve engagement and participation in mathematics learning?

How serious a matter is mathophobia – in relation to your teaching and children's learning, and in relation to wider social well-being?

(*Continued*)

What are your own aims for teaching mathematics? What is the relative importance of each of these aims for you, and for the students that you teach?

Do your aims vary depending upon which class you are working with? If so, why is this and what are the differences?

SIX CURRICULUM OBJECTIVES

Paul Ernest has written extensively about the philosophy of mathematics education. As reported towards the end of Chapter 3, he identified five competing interests in the design of the original mathematics National Curriculum (Ernest, 1991; 1992). These groups had, and still have, different aims for mathematics teaching and learning and the curriculum. His more recent summary of these aims (Ernest, 2004: 316) is as follows:

1   Acquiring basic mathematical skills and numeracy and social training in obedience (authoritarian, basic skills centred)
2   Learning basic skills to solve practical problems with mathematics (industry and work centred)
3   Understanding, and capable in, advanced mathematics, with some appreciation of mathematics (pure mathematics centred)
4   Confidence, creativity and self-expression through mathematics (child-centred progressivist)
5   Empowerment of the learner as highly numerate critical citizen in society (empowerment of social justice concerns).

Ernest proceeds to explain that if the negative connotations are removed and the aims viewed as complementary, they would provide a good basis for core objectives for teaching and learning mathematics. He also added a sixth aim to get a final list of six objectives:

- utilitarian knowledge
- practical, work-related knowledge
- advanced specialist knowledge
- appreciation of mathematics
- mathematical confidence
- social empowerment through mathematics.

This is a useful working list which raises a number of questions and offers a way of understanding our own personal values and priorities in teaching mathematics.

Questions

Compare this list with the one you generated at the start of this chapter. What similarities and differences exist?

In the two lists mentioned above can you recognize some of the teachers with whom you work?

Which of these elements is particularly evident/absent in your school?

How do your own actual classroom practices compare with your beliefs in relation to this list? If there is a difference, why?

ONCE A SCEPTIC …

Ernest's list is helpful but history suggests that a stable balance between these objectives might be difficult to obtain, apart from in the perfect school with perfect teachers, which of course does not exist. His earlier argument about the competing interests in the design of the original NC highlights the influence of power and influence over the curriculum. Though many liberal educators would support the idea of balance, it is clearly not currently present for reasons explored in earlier chapters. One of the reasons that this balance would be difficult to achieve is that no teacher works in isolation, free from the constraints of assessment regimes, textbooks, departmental cultures, and so on. Ernest points out that the public educators (that is with aims in group 5) had no say in the National Curriculum's design (Ernest, 1992) and group 4 also had limited impact as the process went on. So, our focus throughout the remainder of the book will be on those two aspects, along with Ernest's latterly included 'appreciation of mathematics'.

This emphasis aims to redress a serious and damaging imbalance in the curriculum and in the day-to-day experiences of mathematics learners. Moreover, I do not ever expect that complementarity is realistically achievable in the current political climate, or any climate for that matter, but that should not stop us working towards such a position. There will always be difference of opinion regarding the nature of teaching and learning mathematics, and some individuals and groups will continue to exert greater influential than others. As Skovsmose and Valero explain: 'The amazing similarity and stability in the structure of national mathematics curricula across the world show the strength of the shared belief in the logical power of mathematical ideas' (2002: 391).

It is important that as teachers and mathematics educators we keep talking about the different aims for the curriculum, understanding the political motivations for the shifting priorities and, if necessary, questioning and challenging them.

CRITICAL CITIZENSHIP AND GENERAL EDUCATION

In a similar way to how Cockcroft argued for diversity in relation to learning experiences, we are considering here a diversity of purposes for mathematics learning. Teachers should move away from purely content-driven approaches to mathematics learning, towards process, not only in terms of mathematical cognition but also in terms of personal development as future citizens. Such citizens are not simply passive, obedient subjects but are actively engaged in creating a more socially just, democratic society. Mathematics education should play a part in this, as Colin Hannaford (1998: 186) explains:

> If children are taught mathematics well, it will teach them much of the freedom, skills, and of course the disciplines of expression, dissent and tolerance, that democracy needs to succeed. If on the other hand they are taught mathematics as if it has no room for independence; as if they must never question, doubt or disagree; and if we therefore fail to teach them to respect and value those who have different ideas – or wrong ideas – or even no ideas at all … then we can do more than damage their mathematics. For this kind of mathematics teaching destroys democracy.

Think on that

How does your own teaching and that of mathematics teaching that you know relate to these two descriptions of teaching?
  What kinds of classroom culture would need to be in place for the first kind of learning to happen?

Skovsmose and Valero see education as 'a questioning of the self, a judgement of the meaning of life, a construction of a common world, and a criticism of the given order of things' (2002: 385) and it is this position on education and learning that leads to the development of critical citizenship in mathematics education. The primary concern for those adopting the mantle of the public educator is the deliberate attempt to critique society and, in this case, to use mathematics in that critique in such a way that leads to empowerment and social justice.

Adrian Smith's report on post-14 mathematics education did make reference to the need of 'mathematics for the citizen' (2004: 13). This was the last on a list:

- mathematics for its own sake
- mathematics for the knowledge economy
- mathematics for science, technology and engineering
- mathematics for the workplace
- mathematics for the citizen.

This is very functional and even when you do get to the needs of the citizen, it is simply more of the same: '1.9 The acquisition of at least basic mathematical skills – commonly referred to as "numeracy" – is vital to the life opportunities and achievements of individual citizens'. So this highly influential report gets nowhere near the idea of critical citizenship mentioned above. Smith's five 'fors' are almost exclusively related to the needs of employers and it is easy to see how this set of aims might constrain future curriculum development.

In Chapter 3 I briefly outlined Heymann's notion of general education for mathematics. This is a far cry from Smith's mathematical production line for employment and industry. I suspect that he had not read, or did not agree with Heymann's point that '*Conventional mathematics instruction in schools does justice neither to foreseeable societal demands nor to the individual needs and qualification interests of a majority of adolescents*' (2003: 2, original emphasis). Heymann's view, more moderate than that of the critical educators, nevertheless encourages teachers to focus more on the general aims of education:

- preparing for later life
- promoting cultural competence
- developing an understanding of the world
- promoting critical thinking
- developing a sense of responsibility
- practising communication and co-operation.

He explains these in much greater detail and shortly we will consider how these relate to the broad aims of the National Curriculum. In contemplating these different sets of aims the question arises as to the possibilities for change, and the desirability of change. Changing beliefs and practices is far from straightforward and often creates tensions and unforeseen challenges. This is why it is important that teachers consider these matters early in their careers, although of course your understanding and views will develop with experience and time.

Skovsmose and Valero asked a similar question: how far we can go with the critical mathematics education? This question is not easy to answer apart from to say 'Further than we have gone to date'! Kevin Harris makes this appeal for the development of 'transformative intellectuals' who recognize that teachers:

> are pressured to engage with the issues, and follow the discourses and social practices legitimated by the dominant technocratic culture; but to be 'transformative' they must resist being incorporated by the very system which employs them, and which disproportionately rewards those who remove critical scholarship and/or political commitment from their teaching. (Harris, 1998: 178)

This returns me to a point made early in this book – the realization that teachers are *agents of the state*, often unquestioningly teaching a curriculum that does different things to different groups of young people. This differentiation runs counter to my personal beliefs about education and I am convinced more than ever of the need for the critical educator; the 'transformative intellectual'; the public educators in mathematics teaching. These terms all have slightly different meanings but the basic tenet is the same – mathematics education, as part of the larger system of schooling is inherently political and the sooner teachers wake up to this and start to understand, critique and resist its effects, the better for young learners. This does not mean that everyone will agree on the aims for the curriculum or pedagogy but rather classroom teachers should become agents of genuine change in the mathematical education of young people. Of course, not all of you will agree. One such teacher is Alan Brown: 'I think it's probably fair to say that I have a fairly high degree of scepticism about a lot of the qualitative and quantitative research. I think it tends to be done by people who, with the best will in the world, have an axe to grind' (Gates, 2001: 10). I would confidently predict that Alan Brown would not define himself as a 'transformative intellectual' and would think that this whole book is one big axe-grinding endeavour. (Better a sharp axe than a blunt one!)

SOCIAL, MORAL, SPIRITUAL AND CULTURAL DEVELOPMENT IN MATHEMATICS

Following Gill's criticism of the NC, one starting point for rethinking mathematics education (in England) would be to reconfigure the mathematics curriculum so that children's social, moral, spiritual and cultural development underpins all aspects of learning. Such concerns are not often highly prioritized in mathematics lessons and although there is some excellent practice that develops these generic themes, it is by no means common. This has to do with what is emphasized in schools and in the curriculum: the broader development of pupils or classroom learning of mathematics for assessment, for example. In mathematics classrooms there has been, arguably, the greatest imbalance between general education and content-knowledge acquisition, with greater attention given to the latter. So what would be different if the starting point was to consider what mathematical knowledge, skills and understanding should be developed in order that pupils could participate effectively as active citizens in a cosmopolitan, democratic society? Or, to use a German term, what mathematics education could contribute to the development of *allgemeinbildung*, which involves 'competence for self-determination, constructive participation in society, and solidarity towards persons limited in the competence of self-determination and participation' (Elmose and Roth, 2005: 21)?

The second broad aim of the NC might be useful in trying to answer this question and so will provide a loose framework for the remainder of the book: 'The school curriculum should aim to promote pupils' spiritual, moral, social and cultural development and prepare all pupils for the opportunities, responsibilities and experiences of adult life.' The mathematics NC offers one-third of a page of advice on how the first part of this aim might be achieved:

For example, mathematics provides opportunities to promote:

- *spiritual development,* through helping pupils obtain and insight into the infinite, and through explaining the underlying mathematical principles behind
  some of the beautiful natural forms and patterns in the world around us
- *moral development,* helping pupils recognise how logical reasoning can be used
  to consider the consequences of particular decisions and choices and helping
  them learn the value of mathematical truth
- *social development,* through helping the pupils work together productively
  on complex mathematical tasks and helping them see that the result is often
  better than any of them could achieve separately
- *cultural development,* through helping pupils appreciate the mathematical
  thought contributes to the development of our culture and is becoming
  increasingly central to our highly technological future, and through recognis-
  ing that mathematicians from many cultures have contributed to the development of modern day mathematics.

But none of these things are assessed – and should not be – which means they
come a distant second place to curriculum coverage, which is a content-
driven, linearly structured, heavily tested and examined, competitive pursuit.
Until some of the burden of testing and league tables are lifted from the
shoulders of teachers and students it will be difficult to do full justice to these
broader curricular aims.

This guidance is seriously limited and would not convince anyone that
these are priorities for the teaching of mathematics. There is further guidance
on the promotion of 'other aspects', for example, financial capability and
work-related learning, but this too is overly brief.

It seems reasonable to consider how, through a refocusing on these
broader aims for the curriculum, learners of mathematics might be re-engaged
with the subject. There is broad agreement from many countries that 'the key
factor in discouraging potential students who have previously done well in
the subject from continuing to study it is that mathematics is perceived as
irrelevant to students' lives, boring, hard and badly taught' (Brown, 1999:
84). My concern here is not principally with the 'badly taught', but is very
much related to the relevance, difficulty and interest generated in mathematics lessons. One way of challenging this perception is through the inclusion
of lessons and activities that focus as much on these other development priorities as on the process and content of the mathematics learnt.

In her article about personal, social, spiritual, moral cultural development
through mathematics education Jan Winter concludes with the following
question:

> Are these ways of thinking about mathematics teaching just an optional extra; as
> little more than something for the end of term? (I do not know whether to be
> depressed or annoyed when I hear people talking about doing things that are
> fun at the end of term.) On the contrary, I believe that we cannot teach children
> to be numerate if we do not pay attention to the broader experience of their
> learning. The mathematical skills that are so highly prized are meaningless if a

pupil does not have the personal, social and moral education to make sense of the world and thus know when to use them. (Winter, 2001: 211)

She proposes some ways of developing these themes in more detail and I shall refer to some of these examples in Part II of this book. The second part of the NC aim under discussion, that the curriculum should 'prepare all pupils for the opportunities, responsibilities and experiences of adult life', also requires further attention, and relates to several of Heymann's general education principles. This is a big challenge and has relatively low status in mathematics education.

Questions

What would you include in 'the opportunities, responsibilities and experiences of adult life'?

   Which of these aspects of adult life can be adequately prepared for in mathematics lessons? How?

SUMMARY

In the first part of this book we have taken considerable time to explore the nature of mathematics education in England by looking at the historical and current purposes for the curriculum and the impact that it has upon different learners. Much of this background is normally taken for granted and therefore my main aim was to help you to critique school mathematics as we know it at the start of the twenty-first century and understand how it has been shaped over the years.

The mathematics education that children experience in our schools has been shaped largely by the interests of a number of more powerful groups. The result of this over the years is that certain social groups benefit more from their mathematics education than others. If you are reading this book then you are probably part of the privileged group that not only exceeded the grade C GCSE threshold but also achieved an A level (with its associated higher earning power) and a degree in mathematics or a mathematics-related subject. That means you are in high demand! And you decided to become a teacher.

The question is then whether or not you should simply become a part of this system that re-creates such privilege or consider whether there might be a better kind of mathematics education that will be more appropriate to the needs of the whole range of mathematics learners in school. To question the orthodoxy of the current system is not easy or straightforward and in many ways it is easier to simply go with the flow. However, in this chapter I hope I have convinced you that it is worth reconsidering this position and, at the very least, that teachers should aim to develop more balanced mathematics learning experiences for students. This experience is about more that functional numeracy and/or obtaining a GCSE grade C. I also hope that what we are not talking about is an alternative curriculum for low attainers but something that should work for all children if they are to understand the formatting power of mathematics.

When I first read Eric Gutstein's (2006) book, one of my concerns was that the sterling work that he was doing in urban Chicago might be viewed as only for that group of learners. Why would those not subject to, or oppressed by, the misuse of power be concerned about the role of mathematics in such inequitable processes? Why should learners be concerned with democracy and citizenship or appreciation of mathematics if they can easily acquire mathematical power by achieving highly in school? That is exactly why these other aims (the last three of Ernest's six) are so important – so that those in future positions of power understand something of their privileged status in relation to the formatting power of mathematics. Such understanding can only happen in mathematics classrooms.

The use of mathematics in all aspects of life is extensive but often hidden. A curriculum that values the development of *allgemeinbildung* or critical citizenship, of cultural, moral, social and spiritual development, and so on, can help to prepare learners to engage with their world in a more meaningful way. By rethinking the curriculum in this way, prioritizing general and mathematical thinking and process over content acquisition and algorithmic rote learning, learners might be re-engaged with mathematics in a way that could widen participation and the subject's popularity.

At one level this rethink is about broad aims, national curriculum and policy, but at a more practical level the place where you can act is in your own classroom, in small ways that over time can combine to make significant differences for learners (of mathematics). Part II should support you in this process by offering some examples of activities and some ways of thinking about teaching and classroom organization. This is not to say that the only way in which teachers can change things is individually, within their own classrooms. As a teacher you belong to several larger groups (departments, local teacher groups, professional associations, teacher unions, and so on) and these debates about curriculum need to take place at all levels. I would encourage you to get involved and contribute – just as I am advocating an education for citizenship that will mobilize young people to become active in working towards a more socially just society. At the same time I recognize that this is not always easy. However, if you accept that you are already politically engaged, simply by virtue of your role in the national education system, then it should be easier to consider how you might respond to the challenges made in the preceding chapters.

PART II

The next three chapters pick up and develop the themes that have arisen from Part I. They should get you thinking about alternative/complementary classroom activities and pedagogies. There is an emphasis on process rather than content and so these activities are not simply about helping learners to perfect the algorithms of *mathematical grammar*. Rather they are tasks that could develop learners' potential to use mathematics to interpret and construct accounts of the world in which they live. Some of the ideas could have been included in a number of different places, so this organization is only one possibility. There are clear links to other areas of the traditional curriculum (science, geography, religious education (RE), PSHE, Citizenship, and so on) but I do not believe that the mere whiff of a geographical context, for example, means that mathematics teachers should abandon the topic because it is not *pure* mathematics. School mathematics should not simply be a 'service subject' where students learn techniques which can then be applied in the *real* contexts of other curriculum areas, although there is no doubt considerable scope for breaking down current Balkanized school department structures to develop better cross-curricular learning.

The following chapters do not focus so much on the traditional relationship between science, technology, engineering and mathematics, but rather prioritize school mathematics lessons that 'promote pupils' spiritual, moral, social and cultural development and prepare all pupils for the opportunities, responsibilities and experiences of adult life'. That enables us to get to some of the concerns of the critical mathematics educators. Those powerful groups described in Chapter 3 that influenced the form and detailed content of the mathematics National Curriculum might disagree with such aims. These wider aims are for *all* students but I have a particular concern for those who will not achieve a grade C, or will do so under duress, with little or no appreciation of what they are doing!

Each chapter describes broad principles and themes, and includes vignettes and cases of mathematical tasks and lessons. Some of these are original, others are borrowed; some have been used by myself or others with more or less success, whilst others are ideas that can be taken, moulded and used in classrooms where appropriate. Beyond attributing sources published elsewhere, I will not always explain the difference between examples. It is left for you to decide how best to make use of the ideas and resources or whether to just develop your own approaches along the same lines. It is really important to recognize that as the emphasis here is on process, a resource by itself is insufficient. I have seen plenty of excellent resources used in an uninspiring and lifeless way and other teachers who can conjure up excellent mathematics learning opportunities seemingly out of thin air. They are not miracle workers of course, but have often spent many years developing the kinds of personal skills and classroom culture whereby interesting mathematics can be developed from a good opening question, for example. The craft of teaching takes time to develop and although a good resource or idea can be very useful, it is not sufficient to produce quality learning. For that you will need to develop your practice alongside other teachers. A department that fosters a collaborative, experimental and critical approach to curriculum development is an excellent place in which to develop your practice. However, if you find yourself in a mathematics department where there is little innovation or critical engagement with the issues raised in this book, then you would do well to link with someone, or some organization, with whom you can engage in an ongoing dialogue about what you are doing in your classroom. Departmental cultures are critical to developing a more engaging mathematics education that addresses children's social, spiritual, moral and cultural development. You will need to consider carefully the classroom dynamics, culture, resources, pedagogic tools, relationships, and so on that will be necessary for the successful use of these ideas. We will take a moment to consider this below before getting into Part II.

For teachers in England, using the following resources will present you with some challenges as their aim is not to address some small part of an atomized curriculum, neatly packaged under a single, unrealistically simple learning objective. That is not to say that these activities do not have aims, both for mathematics learning and personal development, but rather that they are not designed for the ubiquitous 'three-part-lesson'. This fits with the general aim of the book, which seeks to challenge your thinking about the appropriateness of current pedagogic trends. It is my hope that in recognizing your intellectual and political work as a teacher you might see fit to question and if necessary transgress the boundaries of current educational fads in the interests of the mathematical learning of your students.

At the end of each chapter, related resources and books are signposted. If you should try any of these activities, or have created others, do share them with your colleagues and try to develop working relationships with those who are also interested in broadening young people's experience of mathematics.

THINKING ABOUT YOUR CLASSROOM CULTURE

At the outset of Part II you should consider whether your classroom is ready for something different. I can still remember my first lesson as a student teacher. It was the start of term in January and the school used SMP booklets (a highly popular mathematics scheme of the day). This Year 8 group had spent their four terms at secondary school working through these short booklets largely independently. I arrived with fresh ideas of class discussion, collaborative group projects, open problem-solving tasks and a liberatory zeal to free these young people from what I considered to be the tedium of the SMP booklet scheme! (It was not all bad but the scheme as a whole was something of a straitjacket in that school.) After 10 minutes on my rather too open-ended task I looked across a sea of completely confused, blank looks when one girl raised her hand and asked 'Can we just do the booklets?' Now I had been somewhat naive that day and have learnt a lot about how to introduce open exploratory mathematical tasks, but I did learn an important lesson. Classroom cultures can limit what is possible. In order to do the variety of work that I had hoped to with that group I would need to build things up gradually and develop ways of working together that would allow me to teach in ways to which they were not accustomed.

As I said in the introduction to the book I was privileged to start my teaching in a school where this groundwork had been done. However, it was still clear when working with children from the main four primary feeder schools in Year 7 that the different approaches to learning mathematics had prepared the students in very different ways for secondary school mathematics. One school produced children who excelled in paper-and-pencil methods and had been well drilled in their times-tables. The children from another school loved to solve problems – the more discussion the better – and often produced quite innovative approaches to tasks.

So before continuing with this second part of the book you should take time to look carefully at the classroom cultures in which you are working and ask yourself the following questions.

Questions to consider about your classroom

How is your mathematics classroom organized?
How do students relate to one another and to you?
To what extent are lessons based on text books, individual working, group tasks, and so on?
Are tasks closed and repetitive or open and extended, or some combination of these?
How are your lessons structured? How much variety exists in lesson content, style, and so on?
How commonplace is discussion about misconceptions, applications of mathematics, solving group problems?
If you could have your ideal mathematics learning environment what would it look like? Who would be doing what? What would be your overarching aims?

Organization

These questions are of the utmost importance as all the ideas that follow in this book are not simply about tasks but about the climate in which they are approached. Classes organized as single desks, rows or groups all signify different expectations for engagement in learning. We know that learning is enhanced through social interaction but there are many classrooms in which such a view is not shared. In one Year 6 lesson the class teacher told a boy to stop talking during his mathematics work because 'you can't talk and do mathematics at the same time'! This raises the question of what it means to do mathematics and whilst we would no doubt agree that one can do mathematics alone, you should seek to make the most of the social learning context in which students find themselves. Not only is there strong theoretical support for this but in the context of this book it is really important.

Relationships

The second question about the relationships in the classroom is equally important. Are there strict hierarchies (with the teacher at the top) where competitive activities (for example racing through an unimaginative exercise of dozens of similar questions that neither develop understanding nor collaboration) act to oppose participation, co-operative learning and classroom democracy? We know that these sorts of activities will tend to be preferred by boys and we also know that they do not focus explicitly on the development of understanding. So, considering the kinds of resources used and the sorts of questions being asked is important. You might also consider whether or not you are the holder of all the right answers. One head of department was well known for not answering pupils' questions – at least not with the answer. He would respond with a question that would in turn help the students themselves to form a solution. This is quite different from you being 'The Authority' on all things mathematical, which I hope you have realized is not the case! Is it acceptable for students to give an incorrect method or solution in your classes? Are such errors welcomed as opportunities for learning? Can students question other students – or the teacher – in order to clarify a point or disagree? In Chapter 5 we began to consider the kinds of classrooms that would be more democratic and conducive to collaborative learning: thinking about these points might be useful in moving in that direction.

Textbooks

In my early days of teaching we sometimes used a textbook called *Task Mathematics*, which as the title suggests was full of tasks. As the preferred pedagogy became more learning-objective driven this text was less suited to the political whim of the day because – heaven forbid – tasks engaged learners with different bits of mathematics at the same time. That style was very different from the latest bestseller mathematics schemes. You might take some time to consider the style of the texts used in your school and question what they do well and not so well. One thing we get beginning teachers to do, and you might try yourself, is to make comparisons between different textbooks by focusing on a particular topic. This can reveal some interesting differences in style, content and quality of explanation (Haggarty and Pepin, 2002). Textbooks in England, unlike in some parts of the world, are not sanctioned by any body of expert mathematics educators but are instead commissioned by profit-making companies and written by experienced teachers. Although well meaning, there is very little that breaks the mould and offers alternative possibilities for thinking about classroom practices.

You should not rely exclusively on the school textbook scheme and at the very least should aim to use them more creatively (for example, Prestage and Perks, 2001). My advice to beginning teachers is always to *use the textbook but do not let it use you*. In other words, do not be dictated to by the few writers of the textbook – who made them an authority on how you should teach your class, that topic on that day?

Variety

The Cockcroft report (1982: para. 243) suggested that mathematics lessons should include a variety of tasks and activities, and you should consider the variety in your classroom. Ask yourself what is the most appropriate activity, grouping, timescale and recording process for this piece of work? When was the last time your lesson included something practical; a lesson where nothing was written down; groups completed a task over several lessons (and so there were no three-part lesson!); pupils used computers or graphic calculators; engaged with a social issue of relevance; did not use a textbook; produced a wall display; did some mathematics in an out-of-school (or classroom) context, and so on? You might find it interesting to compile a list of these activities over a half-term and see what the learning diet is like. Is there a healthy balance?

Nel Noddings (1993: 150) argues that 'students should be involved in planning, challenging, negotiating, and evaluating the work that they do in mathematics' to make more democratic classrooms. Learners might bring into the mathematics classroom their own local knowledge which is of relevance and value to them. This is a considerable challenge to us in English schools but such a position is based in part upon the United Nations (UN) Convention on the Rights of the Child, and in England there are many advocating that students be involved as researchers (for example, Fielding and Bragg, 2003) and pupil consultants (Flutter and Rudduck, 2004; MacBeath et al., 2003) for improving teaching and learning. How might this work in your classroom? We will consider this idea again in Chapter 8. One

72 RETHINKING SCHOOL MATHEMATICS

example might be subtracting numbers in a game of darts. Perhaps some of your students play darts or other games in which numerical calculations are performed mentally and make use of efficient yet informal strategies.

A classroom vision

The final question above related to the sense of vision that you have about your own classroom and about young people's learning of mathematics. If you could start from scratch, what would this mathematics learning environment be like? More importantly, what kinds of activity would be taking place in the classroom? Perhaps you have already seen the ideal classroom, or perhaps it is quite different from anything you have experienced. So, rather than simply looking at the current culture of the classrooms in which you work, you might consider how you would want mathematics teaching and learning to develop. What are your longer-term goals for the kind of mathematics teaching that you want to be known for, and what needs to change in order for you to get there? Of course some things might be out of your control, so focus on the things that you can do something about. There are freedoms that you have as a teacher, which will vary considerably from school to school, yet there are also many constraints. You might think of the first part of this book as explaining some of the constraints and systemic boundaries faced by teachers, whereas what follows should enable you to think about the freedoms that you might enjoy in designing a broader range of learning activities.

FURTHER READING

Boaler, J. (1997) *Experiencing School Mathematics: Teaching Styles, Sex and Setting*. Buckingham: Open University Press.
Every teacher of mathematics should read this book and whether you agree with Boaler's conclusions the challenge to the dominant view of what makes an effective mathematics learning culture is worth considering. The book reports from a longitudinal study of two very different schools with very different approaches to the teaching and learning of mathematics.

MATHEMATICS AND CULTURES

Mathematics is a cultural human endeavour and this chapter considers how you might explore this through art, design, ethnomathematics, and so on. You will consider how history and culture might be integrated into classroom learning in an attempt to get away from simply seeing mathematics as a functional set of tools or tricks. This will only be a selection of examples with some indication of how they might be used in the classroom. There is much more that could go into this and other chapters but some ideas can only be mentioned in passing and you can explore their potential for classroom use with colleagues.

Teachers who want to develop an alternative mathematics curriculum have often experienced resistance owing to the culturally entrenched views of what mathematics classrooms should be like. Therefore it is important at the outset for you to look at your own classrooms and practices, and consider how they might develop to accommodate different types of mathematical activity. So, if you have not already read the introduction to this second part of the book you should go back and use the questions to think about your own classroom culture.

Much of Part I was looking at the politics of knowledge and I am aware that this is not a strong focus of this chapter. In fact, I bring much of my own cultural heritage and personal dispositions to bear on selecting examples and I am aware that they are not always representative. So, in reading these examples you might consider not only your own relevant knowledge but that of the young people in your mathematics classes.

THE HISTORY OF MATHEMATICS

Does is matter whether mathematics teachers know or incorporate the history of mathematics into their teaching? Your answer to this question will depend upon your understanding of the nature of mathematics and the purposes of schooling, but if the aim of classroom teaching is to develop a more critical understanding of knowledge then it is particularly useful. In particular you can challenge the Eurocentrism of mathematical ideas commonly used in schools. For example, Pascal's triangle, apparently discovered during the seventeenth century was certainly known by the Chinese over 300 years earlier (and possibly back as long ago as 1050). No doubt Pascal explored the properties of the triangle in great depth, but he was not the first to have known or used it. Why does this matter? In our increasingly culturally diverse classrooms, identifying for young people how their own cultural heritage has contributed to mathematical thinking would not be a bad thing. Recently a young Pakistani history teacher explained to me why she was leaving the profession: *the history she was teaching was not her history*. In a similar sense there might be some value in identifying and using mathematics from Africa, the Middle and Far East, and Asia. Unfortunately there is no summary of this that would be useful for classroom teachers, but a range of sources can be used so that you can gradually develop a sense of the truly multicultural development of mathematics.

Here is one activity that explores how multiplication was done differently in different countries over time, and why we moved to the modern 'castle method'. There is an emphasis here on trying to understand the methods but the task is also a group task that encouraged learners to work together – indeed, they have to in order to be successful:

There is more than one way to multiply!

This activity might be used at the start of Year 7 to revisit multiplication and consider alternative approaches that have been used through the years.

Preparation
The group completes a short diagnostic assessment multiplying 2- and 3-digit numbers. This is marked and groups of four constructed such that their total marks have similar mean and spread.

Main activity
The class is introduced to multiplication *per Gelosia* (Figure 6.1). Groups work to support one another's understanding and practise the method. For homework students research the method and introduce it to someone else. Their findings are discussed at the start of the next lesson, including the demise of the method upon the development of printing presses.

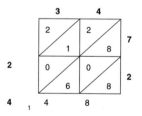

FIGURE 6.1   Multiplication *per Gelosia*

Further investigation
Groups proceed to explore other forms of multiplication, for example, Egyptian and Russian. They consider the advantages and disadvantages of each approach and try to understand why they work.

Post-assessment
Again give groups feedback and give awards to most improved.

Beyond the mathematics itself, this work is collaborative and was designed to remove the competitive element of this kind of number activity. What transpired was that many of the lower attaining young people in the group quickly understood how to multiply *per Gelosia* and were able to support their apparently more able peers. There was no written work produced for marking by the teacher because the peer support and assessment process successful focused on understanding the method.

You might like to find out why it is called '*per Gelosia*'. I would suggest not telling a group how this worked but rather set the problem in a context. My story was one of medieval tax collection.

Examples of Egyptian and Russian multiplication (Figures 6.2 and 6.3) can be found in many places so I only include an example here. There are similarities in the two methods and students might explore why they work. What is significant about removing the even number rows for Russian multiplication? This might lead into a discussion of binary and other

$$21 \times 18 = 378$$

1	18*
2	36
4	72*
8	144
16	288*
21	378

FIGURE 6.2 Egyptian multiplication

$$21 \times 18 = 378$$

21	18
~~10~~	~~36~~
5	72
~~2~~	~~144~~
1	288
21	378

FIGURE 6.3 Russian multiplication

number bases (that is, if allowed – they are not on the NC) and there is a lot of interesting work that you might do here. There are, of course, other forms of multiplication that have been developed, including some tricks for categories of calculation. Some of these can be found at the websites referred to in this chapter.

ETHNOMATHEMATICS

Ethnomathematics is a term first coined by the Brazilian mathematician Ubiratan D'Ambrosio in the 1960s to describe the different mathematics practices of social and cultural groups. '[T]he study of the particular way that specific cultural or ethno groups – whether they are different national, ethnic, linguistic, age or occupational groups or subgroups – go about the tasks of classifying, ordering, counting, measuring and otherwise mathematising their environment' (Ortiz-Franco, 2005: 71). Ethnomathematicians celebrate the different ways in which cultural and historical groups have used mathematics in an attempt to reverse the damage done by the imposition of 'Western' mathematical ideas upon all people.

At one level we could describe an investigation into different work-based uses of mathematics as ethnomathematical. However, the usage normally has a more critical perspective and is often therefore associated with critical educators who themselves often work with students whose mathematical traditions have been suppressed in some way.

Whose numbers?

Over the millennia people have used a variety of number systems, many of which have different structures from the modern number script that is now commonly used across the world. Students might explore the different structures of these number systems and consider their advantages and disadvantages. Figure 6.4 shows some of the base 10 number scripts that preceded the one we use today.

Several centuries before those listed in Figure 6.4 the Babylonians had developed their own positional number system. Students might consider aspects of mathematics that might have been influenced by the Babylonians number system (base 60; they also used a 360-day calendar). They might also explore whether all number systems have a symbol for zero. Why does it matter?

A good task for beginning this exploration of different number scripts comes from Philip Dodd's (1993) *Global Mathematics – a Second Multicultural Resourcebook*. Students are given the grid (Figure 6.5, see page 78) containing six different numbers in each of five number scripts (Gujerati, Chinese, Urdu, Bengali, Hindu-Arabic). They need to identify the numbers in each script and can then extend from there to generate full sets of scripts. It comes as a surprise

FIGURE 6.4   Base 10 number scripts
Source: Pappas (1986: 3).

to some students that the numbers they use in school are not English numbers! The discussion about the value of place-based number systems is relevant here.

Games

Many games from around the world can be investigated using mathematical reasoning and problem-solving approaches, allowing students to generalize whilst enjoying the game. I have worked with A level students doing problem-solving coursework on strategy games such as Nim. You will be more familiar with some of these games than others, and many are variations

FIGURE 6.5   Grid of number scripts

on a theme. Reg Sheppard and John Wilkinson's (1994) collection of 50 such games and puzzles is a good place to start but there are many other example and places where such games can be found.

Shongo networks

These patterns have been traced to the Congo basin where children would draw designs in the sand. Starting at a particular point, each line is traced once only before returning to the start point. You cannot trace a line twice! I have not marked on the start and finish point on the example in Figure 6.6, so that would be the first challenge as there are only two possible points for the start/finish.

The example in Figure 6.6 is not straightforward, so you (or your students) might like to try some simpler ones (Figure 6.7).

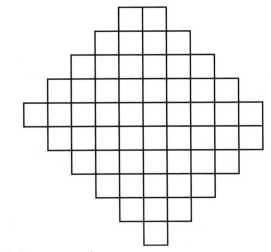

FIGURE 6.6   A Shongo network

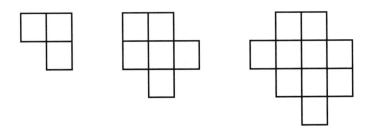

FIGURE 6.7   Simpler Shongo networks

The problem is essentially concerned with traceability of networks con-
sisting of arcs and nodes, and relates to what we know as Euler's rule.
Students might begin by generalizing traceable and non-traceable networks
by categorizing them with nodes having 2, 3, 4, and so on attached arcs. This
would help them to identify the potential start and finish points of the
Shongo networks (most online sources have them marked on but I have
deliberately removed them here). One of the interesting things about such
patterns is that they are an example of how formal mathematics has been
used to understand a seemingly un-mathematical activity. This means that
other game-playing might include considerable amounts of informal mathematical activity and so there is the opportunity to investigate the mathematical rules of other games.

Similar line designs include Drami patterns from Bhutan and Rangavalli
patterns form India. Both are associated with spiritual beliefs, and their
distinctive geometries and cultural significance could be investigated. We will
return later to the spiritual in mathematics lessons.

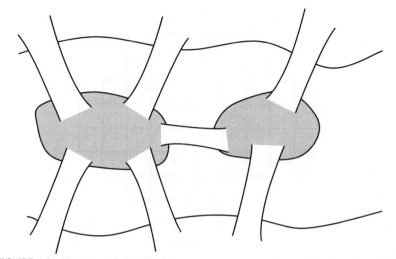

FIGURE 6.8   Könisberg Bridge Problem

A famous problem in network theory is the Könisberg Bridge Problem that prompted Leonard Euler to develop his work on network topology. Through the middle of Könisberg runs the Preger river and two islands are joined by seven bridges (Figure 6.8). The people of Könisberg took it as a challenge to cross all of the bridges without crossing any of them more than once.

Students can use their work on Shongo networks to help them with this problem.

Vedic mathematics

Although there are many opportunities for thinking about mathematics and culture (as well as the link to religious spirituality), Vedic mathematics would be of interest and includes some other informal multiplication methods referred to above. You might already be familiar with some of these ideas but there is extensive web-based material that offers many ideas for classroom investigation and comparison with traditional methods.

MATHEMATICS AND ART

There are plenty of opportunities for linking classroom work on transformations to cultural uses of design. These not only allow for the development of visualization skills and understanding of symmetry or translation, for example, but allow for the learner to understand the cultural and religious significance of such designs.

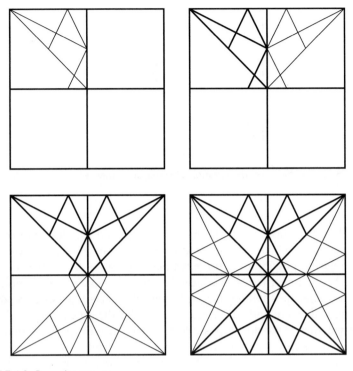

FIGURE 6.9 Rangoli patterns

Rangoli patterns

It is easy to focus here on the construction of Rangoli patterns as a means to exploring symmetry without getting students to consider the religious significance of such patterns to Hindus. Students might do their own research on this before constructing the designs:

- When and where are the patterns created?
- What materials are used to draw them?
- What symbolic meaning, if any, might they have?

The construction in Figure 6.9 is one example showing similar symmetric properties to these patterns.

Students designing these patterns produce quite different results and the discussion about the mathematics of aesthetically pleasing designs is interesting. How many lines should be used to start the design? Does it matter what angles are used for these lines, and so on?

Symmetrical designs have been used in many indigenous cultures including the Maori and Incas. Islamic designs also offer rich opportunities for the investigation of transformational geometry. There are also other

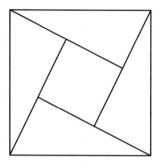

FIGURE 6.10 Geometric demonstration of Pythagorus' theorem

spiritual and religious symbols that offer potential for this kind of work (see Chapter 7). Much artwork that is not religious in origin also offers a wide range of possibilities, for example tessellation construction in the style of M.C. Escher (see www.mcescher.com/ for extensive examples.

Art also offers possibilities for exploring enlargement, perspective, dimensionality, and so on, and you might discuss with the art department in your school whether it would be possible to work on joint projects that bring these two disciplinary perspectives together. The techniques for constructing enlargements are closely related to using vanishing points in paintings, a technique 'discovered' by the artist Brunelleschi in 1413.

Geometic designs, like those in Greek and Roman tiling patterns, are a useful way into exploring Pythagoras' theorem and avoid getting tangled up in algebra before students have understood the basis idea of the theorem. The Chinese knew of the theorem before the Greeks and yet, for both, the demonstration of the theorem were geometric rather than algebraic. How might the diagram in Figure 6.10 be used to show the theorem?

MATHEMATICS AND MUSIC

Why are there 12 notes in an octave? This can be explored using ratios, powers and exponentials, although it is probably the case that the 12-'tone' scale was developed well before the mathematics that could be used to explain it. Music and mathematics have long been associated, with the Greeks describing the whole-number ratios of the scale harmonies and their relationship to string length. For what follows you might need some basic musical knowledge. The scale in Figure 6.11, which I will refer to shortly, is that of C major and you can see the 12 notes from C until the next C an octave higher.

Musical notes have certain frequencies with octaves (for example, the first two notes of 'Somewhere, Over the Rainbow') being in the ratio 1:2. This can easily be seen on a guitar fret board where the 12th fret halves the string length and doubles the frequency to sound the octave. Certain other ratios of

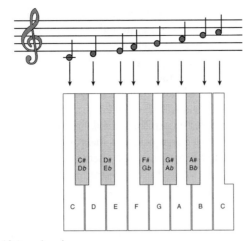

FIGURE 6.11   A 12-'tone' scale

TABLE 6.1   Ratios of frequencies that sound good

Note in scale	1st	2nd	3rd	4th	5th	6th	7th	8th
Ratio to first note	1	9:8	5:4	4:3	3:2	5:3	17:9	2

frequencies sound good to the ear and in a major scale ('do, re, mi, fa, ... ') these ratios are, approximately, as shown in Table 6.1.

Much modern popular music uses three main triads of notes to form the most common chords:

1   Tonic chord (1st, 3rd and 5th)
2   Subdominant chord (4th, 6th and 8th)
3   Dominant chord (5th, 7th and 9th – which is in fact the same note as the 2nd, being one octave above)

If we look at the ratios of their frequencies they are approximately in the ratio 4:5:6. Simpler ratios of three notes are 1:2:3 (simple octaves), 2:3:4 (the 1st 5th and octave) and 3:4:5 (which is really the same as the subdominant chord). So this popular music comprises tones with fairly simple ratios. The problem is that dividing an octave in 12 notes (11 intervals), each consecutive pair in a precise common ratio, does not give these nice-sounding ratios. So when the likes of J.S. Bach wanted to develop a keyboard on which you could play in a number of different keys with more or less the same sort of tune/harmony sounding, there was a problem. Up until then folk music had not the need for modulation (movement between different keys, for example, C major to D major) and so this problem had not arisen. In order to make this work on a fixed tuning instrument like the piano a *tempered scale* was developed, but this meant the ratios were no longer exact (see E in Table 6.2). This tempered scale is a sort of halfway house between what the mathematics demands to be the 'proper' ratios and what the ear finds pleasing. The result is that on a piano certain musical keys have a different sound from others – some more suited to melancholy jazz music and others with a brighter feel to them. Let me try to explain this further.

So, using mathematics to understand this 12-note scale, we want to divide an octave into a number of semi-tones, each pair of consecutive notes having the same ratio. In addition, these need to include some of those ratios between notes that are pleasing to the ear (like the tonic chord which is CEG in the key of C and has frequencies in the ratio 4:5:6). Let us say there is a common ratio a between tones and there are n tones in the octave, so $a^n = 2$. To demonstrate let us take the traditional Western scale with 12 tones. Therefore a is the 12th root of two and produces the frequencies shown in Table 6.2 (the list is not complete).

TABLE 6.2   Frequencies of the traditional Western scale with 12 tones

Note name	C	C#	D	D#	E	F	F#	G	G#	A
Position in scale	1	2	3	4	5	6	7	8	9	10
Relative frequency	1.00	1.06	1.12	1.19	1.26	1.33	1.41	1.50	1.59	1.68

As you can see they are not 'spot on'; the E is slightly over the 1.25 required for perfect harmony. I am told that if you were to ask a trained singer to sing an E against that of the piano there would be some dissonance. She will sing the exact harmony (with the C note) whilst the piano will play a slightly higher frequency. Some experimentation (using a spreadsheet perhaps) will show that 12 is the lowest value of n which will give the harmonious ratios for the CEG chord. But this is not the only value for n that would give these harmonious groups of tones, and indeed there are other scales from India and the Middle East that use different types of scales. This investigation could model these other scales mathematically. This is not easy work but – speaking as an amateur musician of sorts – very interesting. I have not structured these ideas into stand-alone classroom activities but you should be able to see that the potential is there.

This is not the only patterning in music that can be viewed through a mathematical lens, for musical rhythm is constructed using fractions of bars and pieces of music are often periodic. Such an analysis would not need to make use of Bach's cantatas, as much of modern popular music uses the same fractional structure and patterns based on powers of 2. How about a fractional analysis of a recent chart topper? Again, like the art examples above, this work might be linked to the music department in your school.

APPRECIATING MATHEMATICS

Many of the ideas within this chapter are concerned with fostering an appreciation of how mathematics is both part of our culture heritage and used to make sense of cultural tradition. Students should appreciate this and might see how they can develop a mathematical way of looking at the world around them. Here the focus on culture complements an appreciation of the formatting power of mathematics (see Part I) by which social, commercial and political life is shaped by mathematics and its applications. In the following chapters those formatting ideas will be explored further and lead from appreciation to action as we consider how learners might use their mathematical readings of the world to engage with relevant issues.

Before moving on I want to consider a few of mathematics' *big ideas* (Ernest, 2004) that can help learners to appreciate the relationship of mathematics to culture and some of the wonderful ideas that mathematicians have developed over time. In some ways these are what we might call spiritual ideas, and including them in lessons is much more about playing with the ideas than direct application (although such applications do of course exist). The question arises again regarding how you might include such playful exploration in your lessons when the pressure is on both teacher and student to learn techniques for the end of unit/year/Key Stage test.

Fractals and chaos

Through the twentieth century a new mathematical geometry emerged to challenge the dominance of the Euclidian paradigm. These non-Euclidian geometries created forms that retained their level of complexity upon enlargement, unlike a circle, for example, which when magnified looks more and more like a straight line. These fractal forms offered new possibilities for making sense of the world (including the social world where complexity theory is being used to understand life). In Chapter 4 we looked at how this idea is being used to think about classroom learning and to critique ideas like the 'chunking' of learning into tidy, lesson-sized packages. Davis and Sumara's (2000) argument implies that a lesson, or any part of it, is as complex as a term or year of mathematics teaching, and I think this is a really helpful and challenging idea.

Chaos is perhaps best known because of the 'butterfly effect'. Small changes in the inputs for meteorological forecasting programs lead to significantly different outcomes. This branch of mathematics, breaking as it does with the traditional and producing stunning images, is worthy of some appreciation. The following task is taken from Butler's (2004) *Using the Internet* and might be a useful starting point for some work on fractals.

What are fractals?

You are to use the resources of the Internet to investigate fractals.

1   Who is Mandelbrot?
2   What does the word 'chaos' mean in this context?

(Continued)

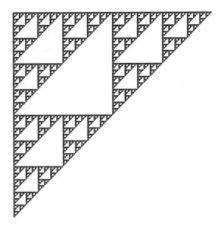

FIGURE 6.12 Sierpinski triangle

(Continued)

3   What is Sierpinski's triangle?
4   What is a 'Snowflake' pattern in this context?
5   What is the 'Butterfly' effect?
6   See if you can download some fractal patterns and design a poster to summarize your findings.

The focus here seems to be on using the Internet and giving six questions like this might be rather constraining. You might instead begin by constructing the Sierpinski triangle (Figure 6.12).

You can do this by starting with a triangle and, by finding the midpoints of the sides, dividing it into four. Repeat this with each of the new triangles, shading the middle triangle as you go, and so on.

For a different approach, begin with a triangle, ruler and die. Label the corners 1/2, 3/4, 5/6 to relate to the six possible die throws. Start from a corner and roll the die to select another corner. Plot a (good-sized) point halfway between the current point and the corner. Repeat, starting from the new point. What happens? Why?

Why will some portions of the triangle never be covered using this second method? What happens if you could magnify the triangle indefinitely and continue the process? This would then lead into a discussion about fractals and what else they might have seen or know about these geometries. They might take this further to explore the relationship between Sierpinski and the Chinese triangle. This work leads to iterative sequences, the notions of convergence, divergence and infinity.

The Koch Snowflake curve (Figure 6.13) is helpful here as you can easily show how the length of curve increases indefinitely whilst the area quickly approaches a limit. Why not make pop-up fractal cards and explore the same issues with volume and surface area?

Similar iterative processes like 'curves or pursuit' offer rich opportunities for mathematical investigation. Four pursuers, let us call them dogs, start at

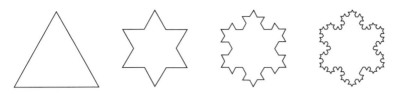

FIGURE 6.13 Koch snowflake curve

each corner of a square, intent upon catching the dog in the next corner (in a clockwise direction). After they have moved a distance (students might draw this as 1 cm) they need to change direction as their target has moved. The curve of pursuit (Figure 6.14) marks out the path travelled by the four pursuing dogs. You might get A level student to use a programming language like LOGO to generate these curves, which might require them to make use of the sine and cosine rules.

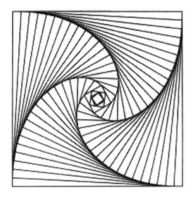

FIGURE 6.14 Curve of pursuit

Special numbers

Are some numbers more special than others? The prime numbers could make such a claim and have a fascinating history. Moreover there are sometimes rich pickings for those who can solve one of prime number theory's enduring puzzles: Goldbach's conjecture (all positive integers greater than or equal to four can be expressed as the sum of two primes). A million dollar prize was offered by Faber and Faber for a successful proof of the conjecture between 20 March 2000 and 20 March 2002. It went unclaimed but it is a very easy conjecture to explain to school students. How might they begin to explain why it works? What would they need to show? Many young people could begin to explore this problem; and the idea that mathematicians might earn 'big bucks' for solving hard mathematics problems is quite an education to them.

The transcendentals e and π could also make claims to being special, each having their own interesting history and applications. The complex or imaginary numbers are also pretty weird and worthy of some thought as they are not easy to imagine (Mazur, 2003). Of course π is known to many school learners but often only in the context of repetitious circle calculations.

David Blatner's *The Joy of Pi* (1997) is an unusual book that takes a look at our relationship with this number. It would be a good book to have around in the classroom, either to refer to or for students to read.

Another fascinating number is φ (phi) or the golden ratio, which also has a rich cultural history and relations to the arts and nature. There are many posters available showing pineapple or sunflower spirals relating to the so-called Fibonacci sequence. From such a simple beginning as

1	1	2	3	5	8	13	21	34	55

all manner of patterns in nature and art can be explored. This sequence played an important role in Dan Brown's book and subsequent film, *The Da Vinci Code*, and it might be worth considering taking a film like this and using clips of it as an introduction to exploring the properties of the sequence and the related golden ratio (see also Livio, 2002). The Vitruvian man (Figure 6.15) could be used to explore this golden ratio and critique classical notions of proportion, aesthetics and beauty (see the Barbie activity in the following chapter.)

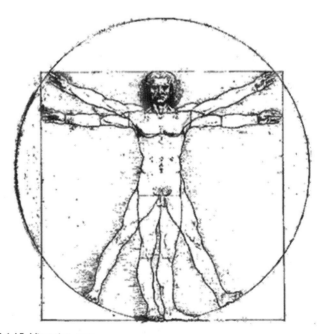

FIGURE 6.15 Vitruvian man

Again there are a myriad of good online sources for exploring the golden ratio. Try, for example, the website of Ron Knott at the University of Surrey (www.mcs.surrey.ac.uk/Personal/R.Knott/Fibonacci/fib.html). It would also be good to have some of these naturally occurring examples of the spirals for students to investigate, for example, the romanesco pictured in Figure 6.16, which also has interesting fractal properties.

FIGURE 6.16   Romanesco

Infinity

The notion of infinity is of much interest to many young children but rarely gets discussed in mathematics lessons. There is something spiritual about pondering the infinite, infinitesimals and zero. Explorations in geometry (possibly hyperbolic geometry) and art allows for such consideration, as does work on the limiting processes related to fractals, for example. The importance of these ideas in many mathematical problems makes them worthy of some consideration and a number of so-called 'popular' books offer historical and cultural views of such mathematical developments.

SUMMARY

As I said in the introduction to this chapter, it would be impossible to get very far into any one area of mathematics and culture in great detail. Rather, my first aim is to encourage you to think for yourself about some of the interesting relationships between mathematics, art, history and human culture, and to begin to consider where in the crowded curriculum you might begin to include some of these ideas and approaches. In some ways this chapter is rather indulgent and some of the mathematics is left a long way from what might be directly usable in the classroom (depending upon your classroom culture of course). You might well be aware of other links that I have not referred to here and I include below details of some sources that might be of further interest. In order to build your repertoire of activities related to culture and mathematics, you should begin to gather together examples, physical objects, films, images and other useful artefacts. You might be in a school where all this currently exists (or is hidden away in a dusty cupboard) or you might need to start building this up for yourself, designing your own tasks and lessons.

One question that we need to ask ourselves is, whose culture are we exploring? To what extent should exploring mathematics in culture include those young people's own knowledge? Hoyles and Noss (2000: 155) make the point that some attempts to incorporate cultural relevance into mathematics teaching runs the risk of becoming patronizing and ends up with activities that are not really that mathematical. They were not impressed by the idea of using fantasy football to develop numeracy, and write: 'Children dislike being patronized, they know only too well what is really required of school mathematics and some will want to know whether the mathematics classes of Winchester and Westminster will be similarly preoccupied' (Hoyles and Noss, 2000: 155). I can safely say that of the thousands of young people I have taught mathematics, none have wanted to know this. However, the point about appropriateness is well made and reflects some of the discussion from Part I.

USEFUL SOURCES AND REFERENCES

Ethnomathematics Digital Library, www.ethnomath.org/index.asp
This web-based directory of around 700 sources is so extensive it is difficult to know where to begin. It is a helpful site for stimulating your own understanding of mathematics is a variety of cultural contexts but there are also many ideas for classroom activities.

The MacTutor History of Mathematics Archive, www-history.mcs. st-andrews.ac.uk/history/
This site offers a comprehensive set of articles on the history of mathematical topics, mathematics and a section on famous curves. It is all very interesting but there are no ready-made classroom resources available.

There is an ever-expanding range of books that seek to present mathematics and the history of mathematical ideas in accessible form. We ask all of our beginning teachers to read such a book and here are some examples that you might find interesting:

Blatner, D. (1997) *The Joy of Pi*. London: Penguin Books.
Jones, L. (ed.) (1991) *Teaching Mathematics and Art*. Cheltenham: Stanley Thorne.
Kaplan, R. and Kaplan, E. (2003) *The Art of the Infinite: Our Lost Language of Numbers*. London: Allen Lane.
Livio, M. (2002) *The Golden Ratio: The Story of Phi, the Extraordinary Number of Nature, Art and Beauty*. Chatham: Review.
Maor, E. (1994) *e: The Story of a Number*. Princeton, NJ: Princeton University Press.
Mazur, B. (2003) *Imagining Numbers (Particularly the Square Root of Minus Fifteen)*. London. Penguin Books.
Sautoy, M. du (2003) *The Music of the Primes: Why an Unsolved Problem in Mathematics Matters*. London: Fourth Estate.
Siefe, C. (2000) *Zero: The Biography of a Dangerous Idea*. London: Souvenir Press.

MATHEMATICS AND SOCIETY

This chapter considers how we might help young people use mathematics to make sense of the society and world in which they live. We start to consider how the construction and focus of tasks helps learners to look at aspects of society in a different way. This way of doing school mathematics might be described as critical (and we have seen that there are a number of proponents of such an approach to the curriculum, both in the UK and elsewhere). There is a strong emphasis here on how we use quantitative data to make sense of our social environment.

The example tasks are aimed at developing mathematical skills and understanding but at the same time should enable students to think about the society in which they live. The amount of data that is readily available for such use is considerable but often bypassed in favour of rather meaningless textbook examples (for example, surveying favourite crisp flavours). In addition, this data can be current and found in daily newspapers or magazines, for example. Interrogating these data sets cannot be done without some engagement with the context but teachers often are concerned about getting side-tracked. It is precisely this overlap between mathematics and social context that we will explore here. Using statistics to better understand the uneven distribution of the world's resources, or probability to explore the nature of gambling (for example, lottery games) are things that mathematicians are well placed to do.

MODELLING SOCIETY

Many mathematics educators recognize the importance of mathematical modelling in society and in the workplace. Such mathematics often requires that relatively low-level mathematical content be used in a fairly sophisticated way. It might well be that your own use of mathematics outside the classroom includes some kind of modelling processes. The National Curriculum Using and Applying mathematics (Ma1) strand should support the development of such modelling work in the classroom but many mathematics classrooms rarely offer opportunities for the kinds of modelling processes that learners might come across in the future. You would be forgiven for not noticing Ma1 in the NC as it is in the small print at the side of the main learning objectives. However, the processes and skills of using and applying mathematics, in this context for modelling, do not generally get learnt by accident. Well in some sense they might, but if we know that people use mathematics in these sorts of ways then surely it makes sense to spend time teaching and learning such skills. The NC does emphasize the problem-solving process when teaching Handling Data, but in reality most children's experience is to acquire a set of data representation and interpretation tools and rarely to apply these to a problem of interest – to them!

In their discussion of 'powerful mathematical ideas' Skovsmose and Valero (2002) describe how salmonella outbreaks in Denmark (which was a national concern) could be modelled mathematically in the classroom. Using 500 film canisters as 'eggs' they infected 50 such eggs by inserting a blue cube, putting a healthy yellow cube into the remaining 450 canisters. Students then sampled 'boxes' of 10 eggs to model the likelihood of infection. What would you expect to happen? Perhaps you could try this out with a group.

A science colleague models the spread of HIV infection, using chemicals, as part of sex and relationships education. Students each have an amount of colourless liquid. However, these colourless liquids are not all the same as some are unknowingly 'infected'. This is only made visible through a simple chemical test. Students then model various patterns of sexual activity through the exchange and intermingling of these colourless fluids and at the end of the time there is a test to see how the infection has spread. Although you might not want to use chemicals in the mathematics classroom it might be worth exploring the possibilities of cross-curricular work. Another related issue that has recently been in the news is the ongoing controversy surrounding the Measles/Mumps/Rubella (MMR) vaccination.

In the last few years doubts have been expressed about the MMR vaccinations. Consequently, some parents have opted to not have their children immunized. This trend is more prevalent in some parts of the country, and in some communities, than it is in others. Mathematical modelling is used in a case like this to explore the probability of an epidemic of, for example, measles. Exploring such scenarios in the classroom can be supported by online simulators (www.nrich.mathematics.org/public/index.php has a good example – 'epidemic modelling'). The computer offers possibilities for modelling these scenarios in a more efficient way that will then allow learners to begin to develop hypotheses and test them. You might start with a news article like that in Figure 7.1.

You might get the students to inquire a little about measles and they will find that research suggests that it might be around 90 per cent contagious for about eight days. If they then use these values in the simulation programme referred to above, you can see what the impact of the disease might be. What is then interesting to do is see how these two variables affect the spread of the disease. One issue with such a task might be that pupils then find out whether or not they have had the vaccination, which could prove interesting and would open up a discussion about the ethics of vaccination. Far from being off-putting, this should encourage you to see how mathematics lessons

> **Experts predict measles epidemic**
>
> **A measles epidemic could sweep London this winter as uptake of the MMR jab continues to fall, experts claim.**
>
> The Health Protection Agency carried out research amid concerns that many parents are not immunising their children.
>
> Research linking MMR to autism has been widely discredited in medical circles.
>
> The latest annual figures showed just 62% of toddlers in south-east London, had been immunised. Health experts say the figure should be 95%.

FIGURE 7.1   BBC news article
Source: BBC, 1 October 2004, http://news.bbc.co.uk/1/hi/England/London/3708318.stm.

might make real connections to life. The mathematical modelling actually provokes the ethical discussion.

So, between the possibilities offered by simple computer simulators and classroom sampling processes there is plenty of space for modelling these situations. These are not the only possibilities for modelling of course. The Royal Society for the Protection of Birds (RSPB) offers some data for A level students to model using spreadsheet applications (Table 7.1).

The RSPB offers a number of tasks that are a good start and get students considering the mathematical functions that would best match these trends, and so are best suited to making predictions for, say, 2010.

I am sure that you can find many more examples of ready data that enable you to explore the mathematics whilst at the same time exploring an issue of

TABLE 7.1   RSPB data: UK over-wintering Mallard population, 1993–98

	1993\94	1994/95	1995/96	1996/97	1997/98
Great Britain					
Morecambe Bay	3,563	4,456	3,798	3,116	3,615
Ouse Washes	5,693	4,511	2,868	2,149	2,582
Lower Derwent Valley	4,000	3,100	3,200	3,655	2,400
The Wash	3,518	3,379	3,512	2,636	2,771
Tring Reservoirs	2,736	3,250	4,000	2,956	2,200
Martin Mere	3,210	3,400	3,100	2,885	2,520
Severn Estuary	3,145	2,870	2,383	3,088	2,076
Humber Estuary	3,055	3,184	2,621	2,112	2,211
Solway Estuary	2,988	2,624	2,637	2,011	1,419
Forth Est.	2,717	2,648	2,003	1,672	1,435
Northern Ireland					
Lough Neagh/Beg	3,699	5,713	8,791	5,399	5,463
Lough Foyle	2,166	1,699	1,755	1,795	1,592
Strangford Lough	1,780	1,886	1,503	1,238	1,753

Source: www.rspb.org.uk/teaching/onlineresources/numeracy/evaluating_predictions.asp.

social or scientific importance. You need to accept that using real data brings with it increased complexity, but part of the skill of everyday data-handling is trying to make sense of this complexity, deciding how best to read the data and making some critical interpretion. Let us stay with this theme of data and consider how young people might engage more purposefully with statistical work. This interpretation of data is, after all, one of the most important mathematical skills that most people will use during their adult lives.

STATISTICS

One of my ongoing concerns regarding the teaching of statistics in school is the lack of purpose underpinning the vast majority of activities. The NC states that stage one should be to 'specify the problem and plan' but often there is not a problem or a question in handling data lessons and so the whole process seems rather purposeless. Where are the questions that motivate the collection of data? My introduction to this chapter referred to the pointlessness of doing a survey of favourite crisp flavours. Of course there might be very good reasons for doing such a survey – if you were running a school shop for example (unless crisps are not on the new healthy eating menu!), or a market researcher employed by Walkers. Either way the rationale for the process of data handling is a good question. You might ask yourself when doing this kind of data-handling work, 'What question would be interesting enough for these pupils to want to find an answer?' This could help to increase their motivation and enable them to consider how they might use their skills to ask their own questions. One of your aims as a teacher should be to enable learners to see how they can use mathematics to explore their own situations, problems and questions.

In a recent conversation with a science teacher who had to teach some mathematics, he explained to me (with some enthusiasm!) how a class were calculating modes of shoe sizes and other personal data. Who would possibly want to know the mode shoe size for a class of 14-year-olds? Perhaps you have a good answer for this, but is it realistic? If there is a good rationale for such a task then the learners should be encouraged to think about what that might be. Similarly, I have seen too many lessons where pupils survey the distribution of pets, favourites, and so on of others in the group. So what! Most survey work I have been involved in has been carried out because someone has a question that they want answering, and that question is normally of considerable importance to them – it is a question worth asking.

Many people in business and commerce work with data and/or survey people but this is not without purpose. Of course, one of the problems for mathematics teachers is that these questions are often not of a mathematical nature and so there is a concern that the mathematics might lead into distracting (perhaps engaging) discussion about other matters. But this is exactly the point, namely, that statistical data can tell us interesting things about the world in which we live. So, rather than focusing again on the mathematics as tools and staying confined within the unreal contexts most often found in textbooks, why not think about real questions or contexts that might be of interest to learners. That is not to say that the mathematics is unimportant, as clearly it is not. Taking a mathematical look at the world is precisely what I am advocating, as school mathematics that permanently has its head in the clouds is of little earthly use. One example I recall from working with a student teacher was a rather sterile lesson on moving averages. Following the lesson we talked through possible contexts in which this idea might be useful and he settled on the idea of reporting company sales and profit figures. So he reworked the lesson and gave groups the task of presenting the results from their 'sales team' to the management. It enabled them to see that the data could be presented in different ways to tell different stories and, although this discussion was not straightforward, they were more engaged than they had been in the previous lesson.

Pupils can be encouraged to suggest areas of individual or collective interest for such statistical investigations. This would require them to decide upon a set of useful questions and then to collect the data themselves. An alternative might be to use a set of data that is readily available and perhaps topical. In that case there needs to be the same attention given to the questions being asked – they need to be purposeful and go beyond the doing of some piece of mathematics for its own sake. For example, what about using the datasheets produced in the newspapers at the start of the Wimbledon tennis tournament. I used this as a way into thinking about equity in sport:

Is tennis fair?

Consider the countries represented by the players at Wimbledon. Compare these with population statistics for these countries. Who is well represented? How does this relate to the wealth of these countries? How might you represent this data?
  A second area of investigation might begin:

Should men and women get equal prize money?
Write down some arguments for and against.
What information would you need to support your argument?
Using the available information (newspapers and the Internet) try to defend your argument to the class.

This project (and variations of it) was one that I carried out on a number of occasions with my Year 7 groups during the Wimbledon championships (although admittedly not all were avid tennis fans!). It provoked some interesting discussion about the nature of sport and the perception of gender difference. In one World Cup year the same group explored some similar issues around football. Newspapers provide a wealth of data in increasingly creative forms and the groups were able to analyse the rankings and success of teams from across the world, comparing gross domestic product (GDP), for example, with footballing prowess. Of course the analysis is complex and the issues are deep, but the process of linking mathematics to current and relevant events and issues was engaging. The issue is not so much whether the analysis is rigorous but rather that mathematics can connect with the world and should do so in real ways.

One of Eric Gutstein's examples ('Simulating wealth – world and the United States') links well to this football-related consideration of global wealth and poverty. His context is the USA, so I rework the activity below for use in the UK.

Show me the money!

This activity encourages students to consider issues of global and national poverty and the relative difference between the rich and the poor.

The first part of the task (following Gutstein) is to divide the class in similar proportion to the population spread across the world's continents. Then, a packet of biscuits is distributed between the continents according to their relative share of global wealth. Finally, the groups representing the continents share their biscuits.

At the start of the new millennium these data are approximately as shown in Table 7.2.

TABLE 7.2   Proportional population spread across three countries

	Population 2000	**Approximate GDP**
Northern America	314,000,000	12,776,478,300,000
Latin America and the Caribbean	519,000,000	4,299,879,000,000
Oceania	31,000,000	737,226,300,000
Europe	727,000,000	14,244,444,000,000
Asia	3,672,000,000	21,504,497,000,000
Africa	794,000,000	2,092,300,800,000

So for a class of 30 students with a pack of 20 biscuits (generous!) see Table 7.3.

What question might you ask them to consider when they have worked through this problem? The discussion will hopefully get to the point where students question the equal distribution of resources amongst European member states for example, and then to an exploration of similar issues in the UK. They can also decide how best to communicate this data to a wider audience.

There are many possibilities for using statistics to explore issues in society and I will cover more of these in the next chapter when looking at

TABLE 7.3   Proportional share of biscuits

	Students	Biscuits	Approx. share
Northern America	2	5	2½
Latin America and the Caribbean	3	2	2/3
Oceania	0	0	
Europe	4	5	1¼
Asia	18	8	½
Africa	4	1	¼

the development of critical citizenship. The examples that I have referred to here are really only the tip of the iceberg and for me one of the exciting opportunities is to work in areas of current interest, either in the news or for the particular group of young people with whom you are working. What you should do is keep your eyes open for interesting sets of data – whatever their context – and begin to think about what questions might be asked of that data. In some ways, including examples of current interest here would defeat the object of what I am saying. Rather your teaching should be informed of a knowledge of current (youth) affairs. As you find these data sources you need to consider which groups the data would be most appropriate for students and how might they best work on the data.

THE SPIRITUAL IN MATHEMATICS CLASSROOMS

I am not sure that this chapter is the best place for including some reference to the spiritual in mathematics. The problem of location is partly due to how one defines spirituality and I do not want to get into such a discussion here. Suffice to say that the aims for the National Curriculum include learners' spiritual development and many teachers of mathematics find it difficult to see how this might work in mathematics classrooms. The example of symbols below is one that might be used to explore religious spirituality but the NC sense of spirituality surely goes wider than that. Mathematical notions of infinity, and of the infinitesimally small, are central to much of mathematics, and even the concepts of zero and nothing deserves some attention as I mentioned in the previous chapter. As with some others issues of concern in this book, there is a problem with some of these spiritual reflections because such philosophical work is hardly the focus of examination systems dominated by the economic priorities of the day. Nevertheless, such spiritual dimensions of mathematics are worth exploring.

Paul Ernest (2004: 323) outlines the following rich task for exploring symmetry that at the same time explores some of the spiritual links and symbolism within religious and other logos.

Symbols

Investigate the major world religions to identify their symbols.
Collect copies of these symbols.

Investigate the modes of symmetry of these symbols. Describe them carefully, with diagrams.

Discuss why you think symbols with such symmetries might be chosen. What religious ideas can express such symmetries?

Collect some major company logos (for example, car manufacturer logos).

How are they different from, and similar to, religious symbols? How do their purposes differ? Explain.

When I talk with beginning teachers about mathematics there is often something essentially spiritual about their descriptions (Noyes, 2007). Anne Watson (1999) describes mathematical spirituality as interconnected with the process of wonder and wondering about mathematics. Again this relates back to some of the *big ideas* mentioned in the last chapter that are worth considering in mathematics lessons.

There is little here that is explicitly about the spiritual in mathematics, and that is in part due to the fact that such reflection should not be 'bolted on'. Unfortunately this is a trend in classrooms at the moment; for example, 'we did thinking skills today so I can tick that off'! What you should think about with many of the themes in this book is how they might become embedded in much of your teaching. Where is the space for wonder and wondering in this lesson; this topic? How can I link to the cultural and religious aspects of human experience that overlap with mathematics during the next fortnight?

The notion of mathematical proof has something essentially spiritual about it, as it deals with supposed doubts and certainties of knowing. It is this idea of certainty that seems to be at the heart of many new teachers' conceptions of the nature of mathematics. On the other hand, such certainty has been called into question and critiqued (Borba and Skovsmose, 1997; Kline, 1980) and, as we have seen, many scholars would question this elitist perspective on mathematical knowledge.

RISK IN MODERN SOCIETY

Modern living in a 'risk society' has been described by Ullrich Beck (1992) as about minimizing risks or 'bads' (as opposed to the acquisition of goods). So we have risk management in schools, risk assessors, highly paid actuaries, and so on. The mathematics of risk can be highly complex but there are plenty of opportunities for exploring such matters in the classroom. The challenge is to make this work both realistic and accessible as in the salmonella example near the beginning of this chapter.

Personalized risk assessment is something we do daily, but is there some mathematics that can be brought to bear on these contexts? At one level this is about understanding the differences between theoretical, experimental and personal probability, which you should be doing as part of your work on chance and probability. So you might explore the issues around chance and gambling, for example. This is about more than doing probability work from a pack of 52 cards. Rarely is risk so simple to understand. One common approach is to look at a lottery system such as the National Lottery, which raises a number of important discussion points that can quite quickly take you beyond the mathematics itself.

Everyone's a winner?

The National Lottery has been running for about 12 years (http://lottery.mersey-world.com/).

Find out how much money has been spent and won during this time?
Find out where the money is spent.
Do you think that the lottery is a good way to fund these organizations?

This topic would also allow you to address some of the misconceptions that children have in their work on probability; for example, that 1, 2, 3, 4, 5 might be more or less likely to win than say 9, 26, 18, 13, 42. The considerable variation in the experimental probabilities of various balls being selected is interesting. Online simulators allow you to explore chances quite quickly, but you could also generate the same process in class with smaller range of numbers.

Is the following article too difficult for these discussions? Perhaps you think that this sounds too much like a sociology topic or would not be appropriate for your learners. However, risk is not just about mathematics but the human effects that result. Maybe this is another opportunity for linking with the humanities department so that both may gain from the other's expertise. Is such thinking too radical? This is the breaking down of traditional subject boundaries that is happening in further and higher education but which has not yet impacted secondary schools.

Who buys lottery tickets? Well according to the National Lottery Commission, it's more likely to be people from occupational classes C2, D and E. In more everyday language it's predominantly working class punters who have a flutter.

Where does the money go? Well the Arts Council gets some of it, and from there it goes to fund joint projects with working class communities around the country as well as encouraging people into theatres who wouldn't normally go there. Actually no, that's not what happens.

Far from redistributing money from one group of working class people to another – forget about the idea of redistribution from the rich to the poor, that's off the agenda – what actually happens is that the money goes to the upper and middle classes.

The Commons Public Accounts Committee found that generally the Arts Council uses lottery funds on projects that benefit the upper and middle classes. Its own figures show that Arts Council supported productions and venues attract a disproportionately large slice of their audiences from the top three occupational groups (A, B, C1). More specifically they pointed to the case of the Sadler's Wells theatre which in addition to an original grant of around £29million, also got additional payments totalling a further £17million. (Independent Working Class Association, www.iwca.info/news/news0018.htm)

Lots of simple games can be used for analysis of the chances of winning and losing but these do not deal with the complex social issues surrounding gambling and something like a national lottery. Such work with pupils should allow them to discuss and develop their ethical understanding of gambling in its various forms.

UNDERSTANDING ADVERTISING AND THE MEDIA WITH MATHEMATICS

Whilst we are thinking about issues that might be considered more contentious, being able to read media advertising mathematically is an important skill that can be developed in the classroom. In the same way, looking critically at certain cultural objects, for example Barbie dolls, might make for an interesting lesson on scale and enlargement.

Deconstructing Barbie

Swapna Mukhopadhyay (2005) explains a task in which students measure Barbie and scale her up to life size to make comparisons with an average person. Through the measurement and scaling up to full-size drawings learners are able to consider how popular culture represents the body and how this relates to adolescent issues of body image, eating disorders and so on.

Perhaps less threatening would be to look at the mathematics of packaging and sales. What mathematics is used to market certain products? In preparation you might start to collect examples of packages, adverts and other resources that might be useful in the classroom. The aim with these is to use them not only to teach mathematics but also to develop critically aware young people who are able to use mathematical skills to question marketing ploys. You might for example look at the percentage extra claims on packaging and whether or not they are misleading. Increasingly there is data to be found everywhere we look and these provide plenty of opportunities for mathematizing in everyday situations. In the next chapter we will return to packaging as we consider nutritional information and labelling.

MATHEMATICS IN A TECHNOLOGICAL FUTURE

Whilst we are focusing on society in this chapter, we need perhaps to think about what and how our pupils might need to learn if they will be working with increasingly complex and ubiquitous technological applications. At one level this might be about understanding the ways in which mathematics is used to underpin many processes in modern living. At another level it is about learning mathematics that fits with the kinds of knowledge and skills that will be useful in the future. I suppose that much of this book is getting you to question the current curriculum model and tease out just how much it is fit for this purpose. The bigger challenge is working out just what would be useful for learners today.

Developing techno-mathematical literacy

The Chief Advisor for Mathematics and her colleagues describe techno-mathematical literacies as 'fusions of mathematical, ICT and workplace-specific competencies that demand an ability to deal with models and to take decisions based on the interpretation of abstract information' (www.tlrp.org/proj/phase111/hoyles.htm). This research is currently ongoing and reflects shifts in the workplace. It is notoriously difficult for workplace changes to impact upon the traditional curriculum, but you might like to consider how your classroom would prepare young people for this mathematical fusion. We have thought a little already about the value of modelling. Another big area for development is the use of ICT applications in working mathematically. This interest will be reflected in the new functional mathematics but will probably not go as far as the techno-literacy approach referred to here. The problem is one of context. How can we engage young people in these ICT/mathematics/modelling processes around issues that might foreshadow a wide variety of workplaces but are highly relevant to their current experience, distant as it is from the world of work? We probably need to look back to those modelling scenarios and work them together with ICT applications. This might be easier said than done in your school, depending upon the level of IT resources.

Encryption and coding

Understanding the use of mathematics in our technological times is not simply about workplace preparation but is also about understanding the increasing mathematical formatting of daily experience. One such area, and here we return to prime numbers, is concerned with coding and encryption. This topic, even at a fairly basic level offers some interesting mathematics but could also lead to an understanding of why mathematics is powerful for computer application and security. The NRICH website has a useful article on public key cryptography, and the books by Sarah Flannery (2001) and Simon Singh (2000) are also well worth reading and having available.

SUMMARY

There has been some overlap between this chapter and the last but the aims for this chapter were more to do with making sense of the society in which we now live. Hopefully, these examples have given you some other ideas of the types of activities that you might develop for your own learners. I am very aware when including certain examples that I imagine them in the kinds of classrooms in which I have taught and now visit regularly. Your classrooms might be very different in culture, composition, the backgrounds of learners, and so on. Accordingly, you will want to think carefully about the appropriateness or otherwise of some of these tasks. Whatever you do, there is always an experimental side to this work and sometimes it will work better than at other times.

On several occasions in the last two chapters I have suggested that you start to collect useful data, artefacts, stories, and so on that might be useful in your mathematics teaching. The more everyday these materials the better, and if you can tap into the youth culture of those young people you are teaching and find out how mathematics might be relevant to them, even better.

USEFUL RESOURCES

Butler, D. (2004) *Using the Internet*. Cambridge: Pearson.
This book (also available as an e-book) lists many useful web-based sources of data and interest for mathematics teaching and learning. He also includes some tasks that could be used as they are or for designing related tasks and activities.

Gutstein, E. and Peterson, B. (eds) (2005) *Rethinking Mathematics: Teaching Social Justice by the Numbers*. Milwaukee, WI: Rethinking Schools.
This is a great collection of writings and activities relating to the themes of Chapters 7 and 8. Many of them are contextualized in US politics and so would need adapting if they were to be used in UK classrooms. Nevertheless you will see the kinds of approaches being used and the sorts of problems tackled.

NRICH website, http://nrich.maths.org/public/index.php
Whether you want to use this site for your own information or to direct
student to it is well worth having in your web browser favourites.

Flannery, S. (2001) *In Code*. London: Profile Books.

Singh, S. (2000) *The Code Book*. London: Fourth Estate.

MATHEMATICS 8AND CITIZENSHIP

This chapter focuses on how mathematics might be used in a curriculum that has as one of its central aims to educate a more participative citizenry. So whilst Chapter 6 was concerned with understanding mathematics as a cultural endeavour and Chapter 7 turned to developing understanding of society through mathematics, this chapter will develop further the notion of 'reading' but also include 'writing the world' with mathematics. Not all of the ideas herein lead to action but they are perhaps more closely linked to the NC aim of preparing all pupils for 'the opportunities, responsibilities and experiences of adult life'.

Our society faces many ethical or moral dilemmas and so you might consider how school mathematics can help to develop more critical and engaged citizens. Again there is some overlap with the previous chapter, which is unavoidable. One of the difficulties in writing about this kind of task is that they should be related to the groups with which you are working. Not all activities will work well with every group, so you will need to select, modify and be creative as appropriate to the needs of young people. In a way these three chapters (6, 7 and 8) have moved increasingly further away from the typical mathematics lesson and so you might find these ideas the hardest to imagine in context. Conversely, it is in the ideas of this chapter that mathematics lessons can become fully engaged with lived realities – rather than with the pseudo-realism of the textbook.

POLITICAL UNDERSTANDING AND ENGAGEMENT

We have seen how mathematics can be used to develop 'socio-political consciousness' that goes beyond understanding political aspects of life with mathematics to using that knowledge to generate political engagement. This can happen at many levels and might be simply about having a say in aspects of school life. But at a different level, if young people in school, as a result of some analysis of data or modelling of some social issue, need to do something, for example, engage with teachers, businesses or politicians, then they should be supported in developing this sense of political engagement – even by mathematics teachers! This is Gutstein's argument but is also, after all, what a useful citizenship curriculum might aim to do. These ideas of reading the world mathematically in a way that might lead to informed action has been described as critical mathematical literacy. Marilyn Frankenstein (2005: 19) outlines four goals for this form of literacy:

1   Understanding the mathematics
2   Understanding the mathematics of political knowledge
3   Understanding the politics of mathematical knowledge
4   Understanding the politics of knowledge.

This chapter aims to get you thinking beyond point 1. How comfortable do you feel about doing this kind of work in your own classrooms? Do you see this as part of your role as a teacher? Your answer here will relate to your personal politics and ideology and, so, some of the ideas in this chapter will be more appealing to you than others. Nevertheless, with the spirit of criticality that we have been trying to adopt since the introduction to the book, I would encourage you to reflect on and examine your own personal view.

PUBLIC SPENDING

The following lesson ideas might get young people thinking about the relative value of money.

What's it worth?

In preparation the class would gather information about how much spending money they earn/receive each week and keep a detailed account of how it is spent. You might want them to record this on a pro forma that can then be collated so that data is anonymous, and the use of a webform might make this easier.

From there this activity could go in a number of different directions: two are outlined below. First, the data is organized and represented graphically (which is where most activities like this would stop!).

Option A:
Ethical giving is currently popular and the Oxfam catalogue (www.oxfamunwrapped.com) offers a range of gift options that can be used to consider what the class expenditure could fund elsewhere for those living in poverty. Paper copies of the catalogue are available but some examples are:

– School dinners for 100 children £6
– Safe Water for 50 people £36
– Essential medicines for a whole village £100
– Create a whole classroom £1700

(Continued)

(Continued)

Question: Given this class's resources what could be bought this week? ... with a 10 per cent donation per annum? ... with our annual expenditure on sweets? and so on.

I would expect my group to be able to generate their own questions and use this to present to their peers through posters, for example.

Option B:
In the summer of 2006 the Chancellor, Gordon Brown, expressed support for replacing the Trident nuclear 'deterrent' at a cost of somewhere in the region of £20 billion.

What is £20 billion?

If the population of the UK is about 60 million, how much is that per person?

How long would it take this class to raise this money if all 'pocket monies' were dedicated to the project? Or how many young people's annual giving would be needed to fund this?

How else could £60 billion be spent? Do you think it is a good use of the money? Why?

This example leads to thinking about how public money is used, and the Nuffield Foundation (www.citizenship.org.uk/resources) offer a related task for use in mathematics classrooms. Under the heading of Citizenship through Mathematics one of these tasks is entitled 'Taxing and Spending'. This three-lesson activity also makes use of a spending diary but gets young people looking at how they pay tax when purchasing certain value added tax (VAT)-rated goods. The second lesson highlights the inequity between income and value added taxes: VAT takes a higher proportion of lower earning incomes. Finally, the third lesson proceeds to explore how the government spends its money and asks pupils to relate their own scales of importance to actual treasury expenditure. There is plenty of data-handling work there and ample opportunity for critical engagement with a range of issues.

If you want to explore these big numbers further, the website Share the World's Resources (STWR) (www.stwr.net) offers some staggering summaries of how expenditure on various military components could have been used. Take for example the Type 42 destroyer *HMS Nottingham*. For the same cost STWR estimate that any one of the following resources could be purchased (this is only a selection):

- 1,446,153,846 meals for starving people.
- 161,142,857 blankets for refugees. In emergencies, families often leave home with only the clothes they are wearing. Blankets give essential protection from the chilling cold.

- 17,747,011 child immunizations. Protect a child from the six childhood killer diseases – diphtheria, whooping cough, measles, polio, tetanus and tuberculosis. A gift of life every child must have.
- 402,311 houses for family's currently living in cramped, unsanitary and dangerous conditions.
- 152,390 schools furnished with desks, chairs, tables, blackboards – vital things children need to build a foundation for learning.
- 30,176,565 children supplied with school books for a whole year.
- 564,000 landmines removed from the ground.
- 14,369,427 children's school desks and school supplies. For children who have no place to sit, study and read this gives one child a desk with pencils, pens and books.

The big numbers of public expenditure are difficult to understand and the politics of spending decisions systems are complex. Nevertheless, mathematics classrooms are one place in which learners can begin to make sense of the scale of public expenditure. On a different scale, Table 8.1 is the 2006–07 expenditure for my local borough council. Might this be a useful source of data to use when considering how the local 5.4 million of council tax money gets spent? The figures over the last few years give some sense of the changing cost of the council. A quick comparison with another local council would raise further issues about the different neighbourhoods. This might form part of a larger project exploring 'where I live'.

TABLE 8.1   A local borough council's expenditure, 2006–07

Services	Gross expenditure	Income	Net expenditure
	£000s	£000s	£000s
Council housing	12,025	12,025	0
Planning and development services	2,677	1,470	1,207
Environmental health	1,051	40	1,011
Refuse collection and recycling	2,530	503	2,027
Highways (including sweeping)	1,265	524	741
Recreation, culture and tourism	5,254	2,477	2,777
Central services	2,460	1,232	1,228
Other housing services	764	218	546
Benefits	18,378	18,107	271
Parking services	460	14	446
Concessions to the elderly and disabled	916	1	915
Other services	1,855	723	1,132
Total services	49,635	37,334	12,301

LOCAL PROJECTS

By itself the data in Table 8.1 would probably be of little interest to young people, until they come to think about their own experience of living in those areas. They could use their mathematics to investigate the impact of local changes, for example. Gutstein (2006) includes two such examples from his work in urban Chicago. One is concerned with the gentrification of the local area in which his school was situated and the effect this was having on the local minority ethnic populations. The second arose from a concern that the police were more likely to stop drivers from certain social groups. Using local data from a range of sources, they carried out mathematics projects to make sense of these situations. Gutstain's examples are well worth reading but it is clear that they are not directly transferable projects. In some ways this kind of teaching is bespoke to the situation in which you find yourselves teaching. Even if I were simply to focus on the city of Nottingham where I live, many of the issues are very different in different parts, of the city. However, a recent discussion in one part of the city highlighted the lack of local opportunities for young people outside of the school day. This would certainly be worth investigation and then the local council spending, and other data like those below, would be more relevant.

Where I live

The data in Table 8.2 compares some views of problems in local neighbourhoods. First, students might look through the data and note any striking features. Troublesome teenagers are mentioned and your classes might have a view on why this is. Perhaps these students might then complete their own survey work on what is good and bad about their own neighbourhoods. They can use the kind of local expenditure referred to earlier and can also get easy access to local demographic information, such as how many young people there are in the local area. They could design their own questionaire and they might cover issues like:

- What do you like about where you live?
- What is not so good about where you live?
- What things can teenagers do in the evenings where you live?
- What opportunities do you think should be available?

They might use some of the categories in Table 8.2 to make some comparisons. Using the Neighbourhood Statistics data (and other data sources) they could analyse the provision for young people in their neighbourhood and present their findings to staff and other interested parties.

Many schools will have pupils who come from different kinds of neighbourhoods and this task might initiate some interesting discussions about the differences. Further than that, it might be interesting for mathematics classes to see how these communities are represented in the ability groups in which they have been placed.

Such a project as this might be unimaginable in the school in which you work. It certainly might be very different from the young people's normal

TABLE 8.2   Residents' views of problems in their neighbourhood: by whether living in a poor quality environment,[1] 2003

England	Quality of environment		Percentages
	Not poor	Poor	All households
Fear of being burgled	41	50	43
Litter and rubbish in the streets	38	55	41
Problems with dogs/dog mess	35	39	36
General level of crime	33	44	35
Heavy traffic	32	46	34
Vandalism and hooliganism	28	40	30
Troublesome teenagers/children	25	34	26
Pollution	19	32	21
Presence of drug dealers/users	18	27	20
Poor state of open space/gardens	17	29	19
Graffiti	15	24	16
Problems with neighbours	12	17	13
All households	84	16	100

Note: 1 See Appendix, Part 10: Poor quality environments.
Source: English House Condition Survey, Office of the Deputy Prime Minister.

experience and might therefore be a difficult place to start your experimentation with alternative activities. What other local projects might work in your own contexts? Start to investigate them and gather together some useful data.

I recently spoke with a beginning teacher who had done some work with his pupils living in a part of London with a reputation for violence. He was particularly interested in whether or not they felt safe on their way to and from school, and this kind of project could make good use of a range of mathematics about the cost of various forms of transport, distances travelled and other quantitative data. As I said earlier in the context of modelling, the individual bits of mathematics needed are not necessarily very high level but modelling this kind of problem and forming some kind of account is far from straightforward. You might be one of those who have said that you like mathematics because it is right or wrong. In these sorts of contexts mathematics can be very useful but the outcomes are not so certain, even though some applications are better than others.

PERSONAL FINANCE

Young people would also benefit for developing some awareness of personal finance. The Personal Finance Education Group is a helpful place to get relevant information (www.pfeg.org/pfeg.asp) and they focus on using mathematics. A pair of beginning teachers reported recently on their work on developing financial awareness with children in a disadvantaged area of a nearby city. At one level they had to explain why having a bank account might be useful as many of these children's parents had always been paid 'cash in hand'. In such communities where many have lived off benefits young people have had little of the induction into personal finance that many of you will have been fortunate to experience. One aspect of their work focused on the use of store cards and many of the students had not understood the nature of interest.

How much?

You really want to buy the new iPod nano (£99) but can only afford to pay by instalments (up to £8 per month). There are three shops from which you could buy it, each of which will offer you their 'store card' to help you pay. They have different rates of interest and minimum monthly payments (Table 8.3). In groups you need to decide which shop to buy from and estimate how much it will cost you.

TABLE 8.3   Three shops' interest rates and minimum monthly payments

Store	APR	Monthly interest	Interest free period	Minimum monthly payment
A	28.9	2.14	12 months	£4
B	21.0	1.60	6 months	£5
C	15.8	1.23	3 months	£6

The students should be able to use spreadsheets for this activity and will need to vary the amount paid per month to investigate the impact. The annualized percentage rate of interest (APR) figures represent the range of current store card rates. Using the Internet to research other offers and make use of payment calculators might also be helpful.

What advice might the students give to someone as a result of their analysis?

This activity is partly about cost, but more importantly about the pros and cons of credit arrangements. Many children in this particular school are likely to be at risk of getting overburdened with debt and this sort of understanding is vital. Figure 8.1 is another example which comes from a Department for Education and Employment (DfEE) circular on personal finance.

The tasks in Figure 8.1 could easily be applied to other purchases, and by the time students reach A level they could begin to consider the costs of owning a flat and of having a mortgage. One lesson I remember well from teaching the SMP 16–19 syllabus was the work on interest and mortgage rates and the incredulous reactions of 17/18-year-olds when they realized just how much a mortgage for a property would cost them. Times have changed since

---

Which is the cheapest mobile phone?

Context

A mathematics lesson for Year 8. The teacher identified mobile phone tariffs as a stimulating and meaningful context in which to use mathematics.

The lesson

The pupils began by exploring a range of different tariffs for mobile phones using commercially produced leaflets collected locally. They were initially asked to give a gut reaction on which phone might be best value for themselves. They were then asked to brainstorm responses to the question: 'What information would you need in order to help you and your group decide which mobile phone to buy?'

In whole class discussion they identified the following factors:

- when and how often they would use the phone;
- who they would call;
- the cost of calls;
- what other charges apply;
- the initial cost of the phone package;
- the implications of the contract agreement.

In pairs, the children were then asked to discuss and agree how and when they might use a mobile phone. They were then asked to calculate the different costs and implications of their own phone use on four different tariffs together with the cost of payphone and chargecard options. They then had to decide on which option they would choose for their own use taking account of the costs and implications. In a whole class discussion the pupils discussed their results and decisions.

This was a convoluted real-life issue in which the pupils used mathematics to understand a complex personal finance decision. One result was that several young people decided that a payphone was much better value than a mobile phone.

FIGURE 8.1   Example using personal finance
Source: DfEE (2000).

then and social trends indicate that many more young people do not 'move out' until they are older. Still, the realities of the cost of life and of owning property are easily explored from a mathematical point of view.

THE COST OF LIVING

Linked to this you might consider other data on the cost of living and the relative earning power of various qualifications. This might be done in the context of considering GCSE and A level options. The datasheet included here could be used in data handling but could also be a starting point for examining equity issues in work. Students might also consider the potential

TABLE 8.4   Average gross weekly earnings in UK: by sex, highest qualification attained and age, 2005 (£ per week)

	16–24	25–34	35–44	45–54	All working age
Men					
Degree or equivalent	356	619	810	862	726
Higher education below degree level	366	501	588	619	554
GCE A level or equivalent	290	446	545	536	470
GCSE grades A* to C or equivalent	253	410	469	463	410
Other (including GCSE below grade C)	253	389	453	435	407
No qualifications	250	325	359	366	342
All men	283	483	574	575	506
Women					
Degree or equivalent	319	528	627	679	561
Higher education below degree level	267	384	464	491	440
GCE A level or equivalent	250	353	421	364	347
GCSE grades A* to C or equivalent	227	330	331	329	308
Other (including GCSE below grade C)	187	378	299	315	313
No qualifications	182	300	235	262	251
All women	253	425	433	424	397
All working age	270	459	524	515	464

Source: Labour Force Survey, Office for National Statistics.

earning power differences with different qualifications (Table 8.4); mathematics, for example.

What questions might students ask of this data? It is important to get the students to think about how they can interrogate the data. Of course you could give them 10 questions but this is not how they will encounter such data in day-to-day life. It is the question 'What is this telling me?' that is the key to developing come critical awareness of the data's messages. Some of the figures are not very different, but remember that this is over only one week. Some calculations on the working-life differences would reveal a more striking picture.

Another data set that might be of interest compares the changing prices of some common household items in the UK (Table 8.5). How might you make use of this kind of data and what interesting questions could be asked?

In using a data set like this you would be trying to enable pupils to read this data and pick out some of the unusual features, developing their critical sense of this data. For example the percentage increase on cigarettes is considerably more than bacon, which is itself more than bread. Why is this the case?

ENVIRONMENTAL AND ETHICAL ISSUES

There are many environmental and ethical issues that we know about because the issues can be quantified in some way. It is therefore easy to see

TABLE 8.5   Changing pieces of household items in the UK

Cost of selected items in the UK						Pence
	1971	1981	1991	1996	2001	2004
500g back bacon	37	142	235	293	343	356
250g cheddar cheese	13	58	86	115	128	142
Eggs (size 2), per dozen	26	78	118	158	172	169
800g white sliced bread	10	37	53	55	51	65
1 pint pasteurized milk	5	19	32	36	36	35
1 kg granulated sugar	9	39	66	76	57	74
100g instant coffee	25	95	130	189	181	175
250g tea bags			150	134	146	139
Packet of 20 cigarettes (filter tip)	27	97	186	273	412	439
Pint of beer	15	65	137	173	203	233
Whiskey (per nip)	..	..	95	123	148	171
Litre of unleaded petrol	..	..	45	57	76	80

Source: Office for National Statistics.

how mathematics can be used to investigate these concerns and below you will see just a few examples of activities.

Food miles

Another of the Nuffield's Citizenship through Mathematics tasks relates to food miles[1] and the ethics of our contemporary food buying and eating habits. The lesson outline which gives you a flavour of how this would work. The class prepare by recording the ingredients of their evening meal (as far as this is possible). Using some prepared datasheets they then estimate how far each of the parts of their meal has travelled in kilometres. They also carry out some online research on the food miles issue (for example, from www.bbc.co.uk/food/food_matters/foodmiles.shtml). This might include the mode of transport to the shop and of the waste from the house. The students then calculate a food miles total and consider how the meal might have been more environmentally friendly. This all leads to a discussion of the pros and cons of buying locally and globally. For example, what would the impact be upon farmers in developing countries of a local food growing policy? All of this work is presented graphically and displayed.

Healthy eating

Food manufacturers have moved recently to identify food values on their packaging. What mathematics is being used here and how do you read it? Rather than using some arbitrary data that has been unrealistically tidied

FIGURE 8.2   A confusing pie chart representation

For more information, please see http://www.eatwell.gov.uk/foodlabels/trafficlights/

and sanitized, why not use this kind of resource (Figure 8.2). Some of the pie-chart-like types of representations are actually quite confusing and worth looking at with a mathematical eye.

Given the interest in healthy eating a good project might be for students to collect such nutrition information for foods that they eat and do some analysis. Say you focused on breakfast cereal, for example, and looked not only at nutritional information but also price. Then questions could be asked about the quality and cost of foods. How much does it cost to eat healthy food? Of course such a project would work very differently in the different kinds of schools represented by different readers, so you would need to tailor this activity to your own context. Nevertheless, there is plenty of mathematics to be done here; admittedly much of it is statistical in nature.

My local primary school has recently imposed a supposed healthy eating regime by which stickers are awarded for healthy lunchboxes. The decision about what is healthy and what is not is sometimes quite arbitrary, influenced by advertising, and generates some devious eating habits among the children so that they can still get their sticker, despite the judgements of lunchtime supervisors. Rather than educating the children to think about balanced, healthy eating it has created a partly unhealthy approach to food. This would be an ideal place to begin a project as it is very relevant to the children.

Related to healthy eating you might get young people to think about the ethics of fast food using the activity in Figure 8.3.

Recycling

Table 8.6, see page 116, represents some figures for the ways in which European Union (EU) countries dispose of their household waste. You might start by offering a group this data and asking them to read it, highlighting some important differences and extremes. What reasons might there be for these differences?

One billion of the world's people do not get enough to eat, yet half the grain grown in the world is used to feed livestock. Why? To fatten cattle up for sale to people who can afford to buy meat. Chronically hungry people rarely have the money to buy meat.

Most cattle today do not graze freely on pasture grasses – if they did their meat would be leaner and healthier. Instead, they are penned up in crowded 'feedlots' and given large quantities of grain. The meat from grain-fed cattle is higher in fat.

For every 16 pounds of grain fed to a cow we only get one pound back in meat on our plates. Producing that pound of meat require 2500 gallons of water. In many areas of the world, people do not have access to even a small amount of clean drinking water and must walk miles a day to get it.

Do the math
If your entire class went to McDonald's and each student ate a Quarter Pounder, how much grain was used to produce the class's lunch? How much water was used?

Explain why you think this is or is not a problem. If it is a problem, what are the possible solutions?

FIGURE 8.3   The hidden grain in meat
Source: Stephanie Kempt, in Gutstein and Peterson (2005: 74).

This could lead to discussion about recycling and our use of the environment. Does your school have a recycling policy? How much of the paper and other materials gets recycled and what is there any gain for the school? This could form the basis of a cross-curricular project in which mathematics learners analyse the recycling across the school, implement some scheme and research its impact.

Many young people are very aware of eco-citizenship issues and it would be a good opportunity to involve them in the design of projects that might enable them to develop mathematical skills at the same time as engaging with a matter of personal or group interest. What other issues would be of interest to students in your classes? These might be internal school matters of perhaps those that affect the local community.

STUDENTS AS RESEARCHERS

The recycling project might engage young people in the process of researching their own learning and social context. This is about more than researching a problem but also involves them in deciding upon a response that comes as the result of them having applied their mathematics to a local concern. The important point to note is that this kind of survey work and cost analysis can be turned back to the student experience of school rather than being 'on' some other situation. Students acting as researchers in school (Fielding and Bragg, 2003) might have something useful to say about their own experience of the curriculum or of a whole-school issue. Enabling them to

TABLE 8.6   Disposal of household waste in the EU

	Landfill	Recycled and Other	Incineration	Waste generated per head (=100%) (kilograms)
Austria	30	59	11	610
Belgium	13	52	36	446
Denmark	5	41	54	675
Finland	63	28	9	450
France	38	28	34	561
Germany	20	57	23	638
Greece	92	8	0	428
Ireland	69	31	0	732
Italy	62	29	9	523
Luxembourg	23	36	42	658
Netherlands	3	64	33	599
Portugal	75	4	22	452
Spain	59	34	7	609
Sweden	14	41	45	471
United Kingdom	74	18	8	592

Source: Department for Environment, Food and Rural Affairs.

research these issues quantitatively would be one way to use school mathematics lessons to develop participative citizenship skills as well as data handling skills. The possibilities for such projects are considerable and might include areas such as researching healthy lifestyles. This is of course related to Nodding's (1993) notion of a democratic classroom that we looked at earlier: young people being partners (though not equal) in shaping and owning their learning.

SUMMARY: A PROBLEM OF FOCUS?

In writing these examples I am aware of how often they seem to be taking learners away from focusing on the mathematics per se and to some other social issue. First, let me say that I do not think that you would necessarily be involved in this kind of activity very often. Secondly, let us remind ourselves that the overarching aim is to get young people to understand how they can use their mathematics to look at the world, to understand what is going on around them and, if necessary, to then take some action. At an almost trivial level this might be like a Year 7 group I worked with who decided that the distribution of a well-known tube of sweets was unfair and so wrote to the manufacturers to question why for the same cost there could be in excess of a 10 per cent difference in quantity. I doubt whether the company was interested at all with their query, and it is hardly a social justice concern, but the process of classroom mathematics leading to a real-world response was being developed. Using data to highlight some form of social injustice is good but the 'so what shall we do about it' is also part of the citizenship education that mathematics teachers should be engaged in. It is this critical sense that these tasks are trying to engender in learners.

FURTHER RESOURCES

Gutstein, E. and Peterson B. (eds) (2005) *Rethinking Mathematics: Teaching Social Justice by the Numbers*. Milwaukee, WI: Rethinking Schools.
This is a great collection of writings and activities relating to the themes of Chapters 7 and 8. Many of them are contextualized in the USA and so would need adapting if they were to be used in UK classrooms. Nevertheless you will see the kinds of approaches being used and the types of problems tackled.

Amnesty International, www.amnesty.org.uk/index.asp.
Human rights in the curriculum: mathematics (ISBN 1 873328 494).

National Statistics Online, www.statistics.gov.uk/ is an excellent source of data but you will need to work through to find usable data sets, which will depend in part upon the group with which you plan to use them.

Personal Finance Education Group, www.pfeg.org/pfeg.asp.

NOTE

1 www.citizenship.org.uk/resources/mathematics-developing-data-food-miles-rationale,1224,NA.html.

FUTURE DIRECTIONS

In this concluding chapter we draw together the discussion from Parts I and II with the aim of outlining a pathway for the future development of mathematics education. This includes a summary of where we now are (from Part I) and some possible alternatives for designing a new mathematics curriculum. This moves beyond functional mathematics (before it has really started) to consider what needs to be at the core of all learners' experience of school mathematics and what is peripheral and optional. Of course, this is still an 'act of the imagination' rather than a strategy for achieving the kind of curriculum that this book advocates. However, at the same time as acknowledging the limitations of a book like this, there is a great deal that any one teacher can do. As a teacher you have a great deal more agency that you might think. After all, every young person learning mathematics in your classroom can be influenced heavily by the approaches that you use in your teaching.

Throughout the book you have been reflecting on various aspects of your classroom practice and this final chapter encourages you to consider again whether you want to make any 'small steps' in the directions that have been discussed.

To foresee the future of mathematics, the true method is to study its history and its present state. (Henri Poincaré)

Can the same be said of school mathematics education? Maybe so, but my concern is how as classroom teachers you can have some small but real influence in shifting that future so that school mathematics education will be of relevance and value to a greater proportion of young people in schools; at the very least those in your classes. If any of what you have read strikes a chord and you feel compelled to reflect upon and change some parts of your classroom practice, then I want to encourage you in that direction. Get together with some like-minded colleagues and begin to explore how to develop mathematics learning that is built upon some of the principles in this book. Please remember that there are no quick fixes and the development of resources and teaching and learning styles takes time, especially if they are a departure from the things that we know best.

Throughout the previous eight chapters our focus has been to understand the nature of school mathematics learning, to identify what might be missing (and overemphasized) and to try to develop some underpinning principles that will guide classroom change. In this final chapter I want to review these arguments so that the case for a rethink of school mathematics is really clear, and then I want to offer you some final encouragements to rethink your own practice in whatever ways you feel most appropriate in response to your reading of the book. It is not realistic to describe what such a rethink will mean for you in your own particular school context. What I do know from visiting many schools is that there are huge differences between departmental and classroom cultures and, yet, for real change to take place this is the level at which the conversation most needs to develop. The ideas in this book come with no mandatory authority and so it is up to you as to what you do in response to them. Hence Heymann's statement about change being from the bottom up, through individual and small groups of teachers beginning to make 'small steps' in a certain direction.

THE PRESENT STATE OF MATHEMATICS EDUCATION

In Part I of the book you were engaged in exploring the social, historical and political context of mathematics education in the UK. It is very easy to think that what we see in practice now is the way it has to be. On the contrary, there are historical and political influences that have had a strong impact upon schools and upon the mathematics curriculum, and it is not a bad thing to critique these.

> It is notoriously difficult for a fish to notice the water around it: and almost as hard, it seems, to see one's own national education system as anything but the natural order of things ... This in turn makes it extraordinarily difficult for politicians, journalists, education professionals and parents to recognise that unquestioned practices are both unusual, and, in principle, changeable. (Wolf, 2000: 104)

A CRISIS IN MATHEMATICS EDUCATION?

There are plenty of politicians and academics who have argued that mathematics education is in a state of crisis (Tikly and Wolf, 2000b). It is not always clear what evidence is used to make this claim as we know that at the same time school examination results are rising and being used as evidence of improved attainment in schools. Nevertheless, some powerful individuals and groups have expressed concerns about the number of mathematics (and STEM) graduates, the preparedness of A level students for undergraduate study, the general level of numeracy skill in the workforce, and so on. These concerns are not about general education or critical citizenship – there is no powerful advocacy for the second aim of the NC, that is, the wider personal development and preparation for adult life. The Smith report fuelled this discontent with mathematics education in schools and made a number of proposals which are now being acted upon by government. The appointment of a Chief Advisor for Mathematics Education and the recent establishment of a National Centre for Excellence in Teaching Mathematics has led to a growing programme of training and professional development as well as a research programme that aims to disseminate good practice. However, owing to the political agenda for the Centre its priorities might not be those represented in this book.

Understanding the political context

The ideological and political positions behind these developments have generally been left unquestioned. The current standards agenda is built upon accountability measures through the public examination system. This system has a powerful influence on how mathematics is taught in school. This perfomativity culture limits other purposes for the school curriculum and does not allow for the space to develop new ways of approaching the teaching and learning of mathematics. Moreover, the need to control the flow of numerate employees to the economy has led to an increasingly skills-based discourse of mathematics teaching in schools. This is now being realized in the introduction of functional mathematics into the 14–19 curriculum and, whilst it is currently not clear exactly how this will work, it is likely to constrain teachers practice yet further at Key Stage 4. The current debate about skills and functional mathematics really only touches the surface of this wider discussion about the purposes of the mathematics curriculum for all learners in school. At the same time there has been the decision to drop coursework from GCSE mathematics. The arguments for this decision are about the reliability of this form of assessment but many educators who value investigative, problem-solving approaches to mathematics will be concerned by this decision. The likely effect will be a reduction in the development of the kinds of transferable mathematical thinking skills that such tasks were intended to develop.

Understanding history and influence

We saw in Chapter 4 that the historical development of schooling had led to two distinct aims for school mathematics instruction: the utilitarian mathematics useful for the world of industry and commerce and the more archaic, pure mathematics of the ancients and of the academy. These two strands are championed by different groups but are still clearly seen in the competing interests of those keen to retain the 'gold standard' of A level mathematics and who want to increase access to A level content in preparation for degree studies, and those who want all 14–19-year-olds to learn functional mathematics. In both cases the claims made upon school mathematics and the curriculum are great. Neither emphasis is satisfactory, for each group regularly complains about the capacity of school mathematics to fulfil its requirements. In the mean time the majority of learners in school find that most of what they do is of little relevance, interest or usefulness.

So these different curriculum purposes are supported politically by powerful people with different aims and aspirations for school learners. We also saw, in Chapter 5, that there might be other aims for the mathematics curriculum but that these generally are not supported by those with the power and influence to make a difference to what happens in schools, at least not in a top-down sense. This is why it is important for individual teachers and departments to think about these issues at the departmental and classroom level.

SOME ALTERNATIVES PRINCIPLES

Let us reconsider the possible alternatives. The various perspectives that can be taken on the purpose of the school mathematics curriculum are not mutually exclusive. Indeed, I hope that it is clear from your reading so far that the 'alternatives' that we have been discussing are really complementary ideas that are essential ingredients of a balanced curriculum. More than that, these ingredients are not 'bolt-on' extras that have to be fitted into an already crowded curriculum but are rather like yeast that should spread through the whole dough. The four ideas that have surfaced through the chapters are:

1   The general aims of the NC
2   Education for critical and active citizenship
3   The principle of general education
4   Pedagogies of access and dissent.

National Curriculum aims

The starting point for this discussion is contained within the mandatory curriculum itself, namely that 'The school curriculum should aim to promote pupils' spiritual, moral, social and cultural development and prepare all pupils for the opportunities, responsibilities and experiences of adult life'. Mathematics teachers must seek to do this more effectively than we have traditionally done. This involves thinking carefully about what this actually means and starting to develop resources and related teaching and learning approaches that will enable us to work in these ways. Part II of the book was beginning to move in this direction, although there is much more work to be done. We also need to acknowledge that adult life is not simply about the world of work but is much broader than that. Think about how you use mathematics outside of your work as a teacher. What mathematics do you use? How closely is it related to the kinds of things you do in schools? What problems and situations do you face in adult life that might be looked at through a mathematical lens, or make use of the kinds of skills and knowledge that could be acquired in mathematics lessons? We have considered how being able to make sense of the complex world in which we live and acting in an informed way in it can be done through mathematics lessons, but this is generally not young people's experience at the moment. Indeed, for many teachers it would require significant shifts in their thinking and practice to include these more general teaching aims. And no teacher is going to want to do this unless they recognize the value of including those other elements. This is why I would encourage beginning teachers to read this book whilst their classroom practice is still developing and such approaches can be built in at this formative stage in your professional development. However, if you are coming to this with your classroom practice already well established you might recognize some resistance to change. I hope I have convinced you that it would be worthwhile exploring these wider curricular aims.

Critical thinking and active citizenship

This application and preparedness for life (and why wait for adulthood) can be thought of as citizenship education in its broadest sense. Critical citizenship allows learners of mathematics to use their knowledge, skills and understanding to 'read and write the world with mathematics'. We also considered the German notion of *allgemeinbildung*: 'competence for self-determination, constructive participation in society, and solidarity towards persons limited in the competence of self-determination and participation' (Elmose and Roth, 2005: 21). It seems clear that mathematics must make a contribution to the development of such a disposition, particularly when data and mathematical technologies are increasingly woven into the fabric of modern living.

This idea will present some challenges to many mathematics teachers. First, this is due to the intellectual shift in acknowledging that your work as a teacher of mathematics might include this aim of citizenship education. Secondly, it is because the kinds of teaching and learning styles usually associated with this work are those normally associated with the PSHE teacher. I have a theory that this is why many mathematics teachers find such PSHE teaching quite challenging. It is not that they do not want to engage in this aspect of young peoples education but that it requires a skill set that is slightly different from that of the typical mathematics teacher. As I said earlier, there are no shortcuts to developing these skills but I think that it is important to recognize this as an issue.

General education

The other broad principle that might be included in this list as an alternative principle for designing mathematics education in the UK is Heymann's notion of general education

- preparing for later life
- promoting cultural competence
- developing an understanding of the world
- promoting critical thinking
- developing a sense of responsibility
- practising communication and co-operation.

As you can see, there are plenty of areas of overlap with our own National Curriculum and with the other ideas in this list. The general nature of these six aims for the mathematics curriculum are clear and they are not primarily for work or for academia, but rather the focus is the learner and his or her own education and personal development. Here again there is the challenge of developing the teacher's pedagogic skill repertoire.

Pedagogies of access and dissent

This dual pedagogic rationale gets to the nub of the point above about complementarity. Critical educators recognize that mathematics tends to filter out people from certain groups and, so, part of their response must be to enable those groups to succeed in this socially important subject – hence a pedagogy of access. Such a pedagogy must work at all education levels. This means that teachers need to understand how those children who arrive at school with the preferred kinds of language and learning resources (which are cultural or economic benefits of growing up in certain kinds of social environments) are likely to do better in school (for example, Bernstein, 1977; Bourdieu, 1989). A socially just pedagogy would take this into account and not penalize children further still, who were already at a disadvantage upon arrival in you classroom. This is not a straightforward task and is certainly more complicated than treating all children equally.

However, as well as these pedagogies of access that will enable more learners to achieve so as to be able to be successful in this system in which they find themselves, teachers might also practice pedagogies of dissent. These enable teachers and young people to learn how to use their mathematics to investigate real situations, uncovering social injustices and acting in response to these. Such approaches use mathematics to engage young people in analysing society, culture and politics, either locally, nationally or globally, in such a way that empowers them to say or do something. Getting involved in such discussion will not be to everyone's liking and one's personal politics will impact upon your willingness to do this kind of teaching. Moreover, this approach would not be about the teacher abusing a position of trust to pedal a message but rather that she or he seeks to engage young people in using mathematics to critique the many 'messages' that they are confronted with on a daily basis.

The principles above reflect arguments made by a number of mathematics educators in several countries. These views are probably not of the majority but they are all arguments that are built upon a concern for the majority of learners of mathematics, for whom there is agreement (amongst this group of writers) that the traditional model of curriculum and pedagogy are not always most suited to the needs of the majority. We saw earlier Paul Ernest's proposed six aims for the curriculum:

- utilitarian knowledge
- practical, work-related knowledge
- advanced specialist knowledge
- appreciation of mathematics
- mathematical confidence
- social empowerment through mathematics.

There is still much more of a mathematics focus here than in Heymann's general education aims listed above. Heymann's six would apply to all learners of mathematics, whatever level of study they were at, but Ernest includes two aims that we have seen are problematic:

- *Practical, work related knowledge*: who decides what that is and is it content based or process oriented? How effectively can mathematical learning be transferred from the classroom to the work context anyway? Does everyone use the same mathematics in their work?
- *Advanced, specialist knowledge*: clearly this is of relevance for some but not for all. Perhaps more difficult is the question of when the curriculum gets to this advanced knowledge. Is this A level or earlier?

That is not to say that these are unimportant, for clearly they are. Rather, they are problematic if part of a core curriculum. On the other hand, all students should have some utilitarian knowledge (let us call this basic numeracy), appreciation of mathematics (as a cultural endeavour and social filter and formatter), mathematical confidence (which would allow them to apply mathematics in a range of applications) and should be socially empowered through their mathematics education. These four aims are the core of what a balanced mathematics curriculum for all should be about. How teachers might achieve this is a different question.

This entire discussion, and some of the discussion from the first part of the book, gets to the heart of your role as a teacher. What are your beliefs? Now would be a good point at which to return to those questions from the introduction. Has your position changed at all? To what extent should you be simply doing as you are told to do as a teacher? If you recognize a lack in what you teach should you reflect, change, criticize, subvert, and so on? This should get you thinking about what it means to be an intellectual teacher.

SOME ALTERNATIVES PROCESSES

So, having recapped those principles from Part I, let us review the kinds of processes that surface in Part II. The second half of the book began with some thinking about the classroom cultures in which you work, and one of the points that it is difficult to make strongly enough is that the rethink of the curriculum that we have been considering needs to go hand in hand with a rethink of classroom culture and pedagogy. As we saw from Hilary Povey's (2003: 56) work: 'to harness mathematics learning for social justice involves rethinking and reframing mathematics classrooms so that both the relationship between participants and the relationship of participants to mathematics (as well as the mathematics itself) is changed'. Many activities in Part II have included some discussion but mathematics classrooms are not often places where high-quality discussion takes place, either in groups or as a class. This is something that needs to develop in many mathematics classrooms. There are other teaching approaches that are better suited to the kinds of activities that have been suggested. Let us consider three of these.

Tasks or exercises?

There has been a trend recently to move to an atomized outcome-driven curriculum. Writing the Learning Objective on a little whiteboard, normally about 1 metre to the side of the larger whiteboard, is de rigeur – like a talisman that somehow ensures quality learning. Now, of course, you want to have aims and objectives for a topic of learning (however many lessons it takes) and you would want children to know what they have learnt. However, young people will not always learn what you want them to learn and might even learn something that you did not plan for! Moreover, they will learn different things at different rates and you will respond contingently to extend some and support others. Do not be worried about questioning the Learning Objective fetish. One of the effects that it has is to hinder the use of longer projects and open tasks. These can still have aims, and such aims should be not only mathematical but also about process, personal development, and so on. Let us move away from the peculiar notion that learning happens in little chunks and is always neat and tidy – it is not. Current trends tend to value certain classroom dynamics and interactions that might be limiting for the kinds of work that you want to do. In making this suggestion the notion of 'access and dissent' comes to the fore again. There are different audiences for your classroom teaching and you might be found varying your teaching if an Ofsted inspector or colleague or headteacher were in your room. One school in which I recently conducted some research had these discussions as a matter of course – how to do 'Ofsted lessons' and what kinds of valuable lessons would not be appropriate for such an occasion. The capacity for pedagogic 'dissent' will depend upon your school context. I often get frustrated when I see beginning teachers' lessons in which they have followed some formulaic approach to a typical lesson because they thought that is what I wanted to see. Surely what young people need is creative planning appropriate to their needs on that particular day, and if that breaks the mould then you should be able to defend that decision intelligently.

If one of the aims of school education is to prepare young people for adult life, then you might question the incongruity between how people work together to solve problems and build knowledge in the world of work, the home, and so on, and the way in which it happens in classrooms – particularly in tests. Now tests are important and as part of a *pedagogy of access* all young people need to know how to play the game of school tests as the consequences of success/failure are considerable. However, it is as important that they know how to work together to solve extended problems that blend mathematical knowledge, skills and understanding with other knowledges and skills. Task approaches to learning are one way of developing these things. That is not to say that all tasks need to have those realistic dimensions, for examples of good task-based approaches to teaching and learning mathematics are available. There is certainly a place for the consolidation and practice that is possible with exercises but generally we are overdependent on such approaches.

Abstract or contextualized?

One of the four aspects of critical thinking referred to in the introduction was 'challenging the importance of context'. The context for most traditional mathematics activity is the classroom in the school, normally in a textbook, often using supposed 'real-life' examples that are a long way from the lived reality of many school learners. Most young people will not do recreational mathematics at home (unlike some of the readers of this book), so the contexts in which they experience mathematics outside the classroom probably bear little or no resemblance to work they do during lessons. How might you change this so that sometimes the mathematics they do in school connects with their lived experiences? This might mean understanding a little more of their lives outside of school and could be done through working on a matter of local, personal or group interest. These contexts as discussed in Part II are not neat and tidy and purely mathematical, but then neither are the 'opportunities, responsibilities and experiences of adult life'.

In this and the other teaching approaches there is a strong focus on collaboration, discussion, interaction and questioning. This in itself is a huge area for discussion and the kinds of mathematics lessons that have been the focus of this book would be dependent upon the development of these teacher skills for their success. For many these are already well established and for others this would be an area of professional development in which it would be well worth investing time.

In thinking about context or abstraction we need to remember again that there is a place in the curriculum for both. Many of us enjoyed the abstracted nature of mathematics when we learnt it at school, and the same is true for many people today. What I am concerned for here is that there is an attempt at genuine contextualization in young people's experience of mathematic learning, rather than the false 'realism' referred to earlier. As not all mathematical topics lend themselves easily to such genuine contextualization it is worth making it work properly when it is possible.

Democratic (or anti-democratic?)

The final theme that we should consider briefly here is the notion of democratic mathematics education. I have rather provocatively paired this with anti-democratic mathematics education. In Part I several arguments were made to suggest that elements of mathematics education were not built upon principles of social justice. My point here is about young people's active participation in their learning; the idea proffered by Nel Noddings when she talked about young people having a say in their education. This does not mean that the teacher rescinds overall control of the group or the direction of the learning, but rather that you think of how you might develop a classroom culture that reflects the democratic society in which we live. This is partly achieved through the nature of interactions in the classroom and partly through the negotiation of curriculum and pedagogy, of project content and so on.

THE BIG DECISIONS

What do I mean by *big decisions*? I suppose that I am really talking about influential decision at a national level. Before the turn of the millennium,

Celia Hoyles and her colleagues suggested that 'mathematics education in the third millennium will not just be about teaching and learning mathematics, but about the nature of knowledge and the place of mathematics within society' (Hoyles et al., 1999: 3). But what do you think they mean by 'the nature of knowledge and the place of mathematics within society'? Moreover, how would a national curriculum actually achieve this? In thinking about the nature of knowledge you cannot escape from thinking about the politics of knowledge, and that leads us into the discussions of this book.

The first big issue is concerned with whether or not the curriculum should be content driven or whether there should be more of an emphasis on skills, understanding, processes, real-life applicability, and so on. Currently, the emphasis on content knowledge, made stronger by the testing regime, stifles much of the other aims for the curriculum as we have seen.

The PISA study defines mathematics as: 'the capacity to identify and understand the role that mathematics plays in the world, to make well-founded judgements and to use and engage with mathematics in ways that meet the needs of the individual's life as a constructive, concerned and reflective citizen' (OECD, 2003 in OECD, 2004: 26). The study makes further definitions that are useful here (OECD, 2004: 26): there are three assessment areas in this huge international study, namely, *content*, *process* and *situation*. The four content areas for mathematics are quantity, shape and space, change and relationships and uncertainty. The processes assessed are reproduction (simple mathematical operations), connections (bringing together ideas to solve straightforward problems) and reflection (wider mathematical thinking). The situations are listed as personal, educational and occupational, local and broader community and scientific.

There is much that is good here that would be useful in designing a curriculum but there is also plenty that is open to interpretation. Developing 'the capacity to identify and understand the role that mathematics plays in the world' is a laudable aim and one that we have been concerned with in this book. How we might achieve that is a moot point. The content areas are little different from what we currently have and no doubt our NC could be mapped into these without much difficulty. The situations are also helpful but what they mean in practice is unclear.

Content or process

Mathematics curricula have traditionally focused heavily on content but there is an argument for a much stronger emphasis in this day and age upon process and the contingency of knowledge. I have already referred to Mike Newby's scenarios for the education system of the future but here they are again:

> The *subject content* (such as it is taught in schools, for it will be available everywhere) will be in a constant state of flux, barriers between disciplines crumbling,

established subjects coming to blend and morph into new ones. (Newby, 2005: 298, emphasis in original).

The *contingent* nature of knowledge will therefore require learners in the schools of the future to acquire qualities of thought and action which will suit them to succeed in a world with fewer certainties and greater risks. (Newby, 2005: 299, emphasis in original)

Together with the idea that the nature of knowledge is changing, we might think about whether the curriculum should continue to be structured in the way it currently is, whereby content is prioritized over skills, adaptability, applicability, transferability of knowledge and so on. In order to make this happen there would need to be a concurrent shift in the modes of assessment and it is difficult to envisage how this might happen, but a world without the overwhelmingly burdensome testing system is still imaginable.

Core mathematics

The question arises again about whether or not all learners in school should do the same mathematics or whether or not there should be core elements and options. This possibility was discussed earlier and was related to the kinds of routes that might be taken beyond compulsory schooling. Such an approach would also take into account that functional mathematics might be different, depending upon what function it is intended to fulfil; that is, what roles the users are likely to find themselves, in the future. Earlier in this chapter Paul Ernest's six aims for the curriculum were whittled down to four and you can decide whether you think that these four points would be a good basis for building the curriculum. Of course you and I are not in a position to decide such things, but we are perhaps in a position to alter the balance within our own classrooms and think about how we might move forward.

FINAL COMMENTS – FIRST STEPS

My emphasis has been on learning mathematics in a collaborative, task-based approach where classrooms become more democratic, learners have more input into their own learning and there is a far greater degree of mathematical application. The emphasis in this book has been on the kinds of approaches that I think need to complement some of the best teaching that children currently experience. However, I am going further than that and fully agree with Jan Winter (2001) when she says that these are not 'bolt-on' kinds of activities. You should, wherever possible, be trying to apply these principles to the teaching of any aspect of mathematics and for any group. One of the difficulties for you is that this approach in some ways stands in opposition to having a textbook scheme that the teacher remains subservient to. Learning cannot be controlled and managed in that way.

How much is your teaching simply a 'pedagogy of access'? More importantly, who does it really provide access for? Yes, it is really important for those pupils who want to progress with their studies that they have the necessary skills to be able to achieve this. However, the 'pedagogy of dissent' is also important if learners are going to be able to use their mathematics to make sense of and impact the world in which they live using their mathematics. So you might regularly ask yourself, 'How can I teach this topic in such a way that the principles referred to in this book are developed?' To what extent can learners' social, spiritual, moral and cultural development be enhanced through this topic? Now that will require you to be creative, take some risks and possibly dissent from the norm. And some of your attempts will not go according to plan. However, if the safe but rather meaningless repetitive textbook exercises are the only alternative, then it is worth a go!

So this is what you might do as an individual, take those small steps in the direction of Heymann's general principles of general education, or critical mathematics, or citizenship education through mathematics. You will warm to certain of these ideas more than others, which is completely understandable. Developing a more critical disposition to your work as a teacher of mathematics is vitally important and this might include breaking the mould of traditional. Who knows, you might surprise your students by working on some mathematics that would genuinely be of interest to them.

REFERENCES

Anderson, J. (2002) 'Being mathematically educated in the 21st century: what should it mean?', in L. Haggarty (ed.), *Teaching Mathematics in Secondary School*. London: RoutledgeFalmer. pp. 19–32.

Apple, M. (1993) *Official Knowledge: Democratic Education in a Conservative Age*. London: Routledge.

Ball, S. (2003) 'The teacher's soul and the terrors of performativity', *Journal of Education Policy*, 18(2): 215–28.

BBC News (1999) The secret shame of mathematics teachers, 2 September 1999, news.bbc.co.uk/1/hi/education/436669.stm (accessed 12/1/07).

BBC News (2000) More philosophical grounds, 3 October, 2000, news. bbc.co.uk/1/hi/education/954677.stm (accessed 12/1/07).

BBC News (2003) Terry Bladon, 21 April 2003 news.bbc.co.uk/1/hi/education/2964783. stm (accessed 12/1/07).

BBC News (2004) Action plan to rescue mathematics by G. Eason, 24 February 2004, news.bbc.co.uk/1/hi/education/351449.stm (accessed 12/1/07).

BBC News (2005a) Students struggling with maths, 2 June 2005, news.bbc.co.uk/1/hi/education/4600783.stm (accessed 12/1/07).

BBC News (2005b) Spiral of decline, 28 June 2005, news.bbc.co.uk/1/hi/education/4629955.stm (accessed 12/1/07).

Beck, U. (1992) *Risk Society: Towards a New Modernity*. London: Sage Publications.

Beck, U. (1994) 'The reinvention of politics: towards a theory of reflexive modernisation', in U. Beck, A. Giddens and S. Lash (eds), *Reflexive Modernisation: Politics, Tradition and Aesthetics in the Modern Social Order*. Stanford, CA: Stanford University Press.

Bell, A., D. Rooke, and Wigley, A. (1979) *Journey into Mathematics*. London: Blackie.

Bernstein, B. (1977) *Class, Codes and Control: Volume 3; Towards a Theory of Educational Transmissions*. London: Routledge & Kegan Paul.

Bishop, A. (1988) *Mathematical Enculturation*. Dordrecht: Kluwer Academic.

Blatner, D. (1997) *The Joy of Pi*. London: Penguin Books.

Boaler, J. (1997) *Experiencing School Mathematics, Teaching Styles, Sex and Setting*. Buckingham: Open University Press.

Boaler, J., Wiliam, D and Brown, M. (1998) 'Student's experiences of ability grouping – disaffection, polarisation and the construction of failure', paper presented at 1st Mathematics Education and Society Conference, Nottingham, England 6–11th September.

Borba, M. and O. Skovsmose (1997) 'The ideology of certainty in mathematics education', *For the Learning of Mathematics*, 17(3): 17–23.

Bourdieu, P. (1989) 'How schools help reproduce the social order', *Current Contents: Social and Behavioural Science*, 21(8): 16.

Bourdieu, P. (1998) *Practical Reason*. Cambridge: Polity Press.

Brown, L. and J. Waddingham (1982). *An Addendum to Cockcroft*. Bristol: Avon LEA.

Brown, M., (1998) 'The tyranny of the international horse race', in R. Slee, G. Weiner and S. Tomlinson (eds), *School Effectiveness for Whom? Challenges to the School Effectiveness and School Improvement Movements.* London: Falmer Press. pp. 33–47.

Brown, M. (1999) 'One mathematics for all?', in C. Hoyles, C. Morgan and G. Woodhouse (eds), *Rethinking the Mathematics Curriculum.* London: Falmer Press. pp. 78–89.

Brown, M., Askew, M., Millett, M. and Rhodes, V. (2003) 'The key role of educational research in the development and evaluation of the National Numeracy Strategy', *British Educational Research Journal*, 29(5): 655–72.

Butler, D. (2004) *Using the Internet.* Cambridge: Pearson.

Bynner, J. and S. Parsons (1997) *Does Numeracy Matter? Evidence from the National Child Development Study on the Impact of Poor Numeracy on Adult Life.* London: Basic Skills Agency.

Castells, M. (2000) *The Rise of the Network Society.* Oxford: Blackwells.

Cockcroft, W.H. (1982) *Mathematics Counts.* London: HMSO.

Connolly, P. (2006) 'The effects of social class and ethnicity on gender differences in GCSE attainment: a secondary analysis of the Youth Cohort Study of England and Wales 1997–2001', *British Educational Research Journal*, 32(1): 3–21.

Cooney, T. and B. Shealy (1997) 'On understanding the structure of teachers' beliefs and their relationship to change', in E. Fennema and B.S. Nelson (eds), *Mathematics Teacher in Transition.* Mahwah, N: Lawrence Erlbaum Associates. pp. 87–109.

Cooper, B. and M. Dunne (1998) 'Social class, gender, equity and National Curriculum tests in maths', 1st Mathematics Education and Society Conference, Nottingham, England 6th-11th September.

Cooper, B. and M. Dunne (2000) *Assessing Children's Mathematical Knowledge: Social Class, Sex and Problem Solving.* Buckingham: Open University Press.

Davis, B. and D. Sumara (2000) 'Curriculum forms: on the assumed shapes of knowing and knowledge', *Journal of Curriculum Studies*, 32(6): 821–45.

Davis, P. (1993) 'Applied mathematics as social contract', in S. Restivo, J.P.V. Bendegum and R. Fischer (eds), *Math Worlds: Philosophical and Social Studies of Mathematics and Mathematics Education.* New York: State University of New York Press. pp. 182–94.

Department for Education and Skills (DfES) (1999) *The National Curriculum for England and Wales: Mathematics.* London: HMSO.

Department for Education and Skills (DfES) (2003) *Every Child Matters.* London: HMSO.

Department for Education and Skills (DfES) (2004) *14–19 Reform Final Report.* London: Department for Education and Skills.

Department for Education and Skills (DfES) (2005) *14–19 Education and Skills.* London: HMSO.

Department for Education and Employment (DfEE) (2000) *Financial Capability through Personal Finance Education.* London: DfEE.

Department of Education and Science (DES) (1982) *Mathematics Counts.* London: HMSO.

Dewey, J. (1916) *Democracy and Education: An Introduction to the Philosophy of Education.* New York: Macmillan.

Dodds, P. (1993) *Global Mathematics: A Second Cultural Resourcebook.* Manchester: DEP.

Dowling, P. and R. Noss (eds) (1990) *Mathematics versus the National Curriculum.* London: Falmer Press.

Edmonds, B. and D. Ball (1988) 'Looking for relevance: can we let them decide?', in D. Pimm (ed.), *Mathematics Teachers and Children.* Sevenoaks: Hodder and Stoughton. pp. 126–8.

Elmose, S. and W.-M. Roth (2005) '*Allgemeinbildung*: readiness for living in risk-society', *Journal of Curriculum Studies,* 37(1): 11–34.

Ernest, P. (1991) *The Philosophy of Mathematics Education*. Basingstoke: Falmer Press.

Ernest, P. (1992) 'The National Curriculum in mathematics: political perspectives and implications', in S. Lerman and M. Nickson (eds), *The Social Context of Mathematics Education: Theory and Practice*. London: South Bank Press. pp. 33–61.

Ernest, P. (2004) 'Relevance versus utility: some ideas on what it means to know mathematics', in B. Clarke, D. Clarke, G. Emanuelsson, B. Johansson, D. Lambdin, F. Lester, A. Wallby, and K. Wallby (eds), *International Perspectives on Learning and Teaching Mathematics*. Goteborg: National Centre for Mathematics Education. pp. 313–27.

Fennema, E. and G. Leder (1990) *Mathematics and Gender: Influences on Teachers and Students*. New York: Teachers College Press.

Fielding, M. and S. Bragg (2003) *Students as Researchers: Making a Difference*. Cambridge: Pearson.

Flannery, S. (2001) *In Code*. London: Profile Books.

Flutter, J. and J. Rudduck (2004) *Consulting Pupils: What's in It for Schools*. London: RoutledgeFalmer.

Frankenstein, M. (2005) 'Reading the world with math', in E. Gutstein and B. Peterson (eds), *Rethinking Mathematics: Teaching Social Justice by the Numbers*. Milwaukee, WI: Rethinking Schools. pp. 19–30.

Freudenthal, H. (1991) *Revisiting Mathematics Education*. Dordrecht: Kluwer Academic.

Friere, P. (1972) *Pedagogy of the Oppressed*. Harmondsworth: Penguin Books.

Galton, M., C. Comber, and T. Pell. (2002) 'The consequences of transfer for pupils: attitudes and attainment', in L. Hargreaves and M. Galton (eds), *Transfer from the Primary Classroom: 20 Years on*. London: RoutledgeFalmer. pp. 131–58.

Gates, P. (ed.) (2001) *Issues in Mathematics Teaching*. London: RoutledgeFalmer.

Gill, P. (2004) 'Mathematics', in J. White (ed.), *Rethinking the School Curriculum. Values, Aims and Purposes*. London: RoutlegeFalmer. pp. 104–16.

Gutstein, E. (2006) *Reading and Writing the World with Mathematics: Toward a Pedagogy for Social Justice*. New York: Routledge.

Gutstein, E. and B. Peterson (eds) (2005) *Rethinking Mathematics: Teaching Social Justice by the Numbers*. Milwaukee, WI: Rethinking Schools.

Haggarty, L. and B. Pepin (2002) 'An investigation of mathematics textbooks and their use in English, French and German classrooms: who gets an opportunity to learn what?', *British Educational Research Journal*, 28(4): 567–90.

Hannaford, C. (1998) 'Mathematics teaching *is* democratic education', *Zentralblatt für Didaktic der Mathematik/International Reviews on Mathematics Education*, 30(6): 181–7.

Hardy, G.H. (1941) *A Mathematician's Apology*. London: Cambridge University Press.

Harris, K. (1998) 'Mathematics teachers as democratic agents', *Zentralblatt für Didaktic der Mathematik/International Reviews on Mathematics Education*, 30(6): 174–80.

Heymann, H.W. (2003) *Why Teach Mathematics: A Focus on General Education*. Dordrecht: Kluwer.

Howson, G. and B. Wilson (eds) (1986) *School Mathematics in the 1990s*. Cambridge: Cambridge University Press.

Hoyles, C. and R. Noss (2000) 'Facts and Fantasies: what mathematics should our children learn?', in C. Tikly and A. Wolf (eds), *The Mathematics We Need Now: Demands, Deficits and Remedies*. London: Institute of Education. pp. 154–74.

Hoyles, C., C. Morgan and G. Woodhouse (eds) (1999) *Rethinking the Mathematics Curriculum*. London: Falmer Press.

Jones, L. (ed.) (1991) *Teaching Mathematics and Art*. Cheltenham: Stanley Thorne.

Kaplan, R. and E. Kaplan (2003) *The Art of the Infinite: Our Lost Language of Numbers*. London: Allen Lane.

Kassem, D. (2001) 'Ethnicity and mathematics education', in P. Gates (ed.), *Issues in Mathematics Teaching*. London: RoutledgeFalmer. pp. 64–76.

Kilpatrick, J. and G.M.A. Stanic (1995) 'Paths to the present', in I. M. Carl (ed.), *Seventy-five Years of Progress: Prospects for School Mathematics*. Reston, VA: National Council of Teachers of Mathematics. pp. 3–20.

Kline, M. (1980) *Mathematics: The Loss of Certainty*. Oxford: Oxford University Press.

Lakoff, G. and R. Nunez (2000) *Where Mathematics Comes From*. New York: Basic Books.

Lerman, S. (1990) 'Alternative perspectives of the nature of mathematics and their influence on the teaching of mathematics', *British Educational Research Journal*, 16(1): 53–61.

Livio, M. (2002) *The Golden Ratio: The Story of Phi, the Extraordinary Number of Nature, Art and Beauty*. Chatham: Review.

MacBeath, J., H. Demetriou, J. Rudduck, and K. Myers, (2003) *Consulting Pupils: A Toolkit for Teachers*. Cambridge: Pearson.

Maor, E. (1994) *e: The Story of a Number*. Princeton, NJ: Princeton University Press.

Mazur, B. (2003) *Imagining Numbers (Particularly the Square Root of Minus Fifteen)*. London: Penguin Books.

Mendick, H. (2004) *A Mathematician Goes to the Movies*. Informal Proceedings British Society for Research into Learning Mathematics, 24(1): 43–48.

Mendick, H. (2005) 'Mathematical stories: why do more boys than girls choose to study mathematics at AS-level in England?', *British Journal of Sociology of Education*, 26(2): 235–51.

Mukhopadhyay, S. (2005) 'Deconstructing Barbie', in E. Gutstein and B. Peterson (eds), *Rethinking Mathematics: Teaching Social Justice by the Numbers*. Milwaukee, WI: Rethinking Schools. pp. 122–3.

Nardi, E. and S. Steward (2003) 'Is mathematics T.I.R.E.D? A profile of quiet dis-affection in the secondary mathematics classroom', *British Educational Research Journal*, 29(3): 345–67.

Newby, M. (2005) 'A curriculum for 2020', *Journal of Education for Teaching*, 31(4): 297–300.

Noddings, N. (1993) 'Politicizing the mathematics classroom', in S. Restivo, J.P.V. Bendegum and R. Fischer (eds), *Math Worlds*. Albany, NY: SUNY Press. pp. 150–61.

Noddings, N. (2004) '*Mathematics, Culture and Equity*. San Diego, CA: American Education Research Assocation.

Noss, R. (2002) 'Mathematics in the digital technology age', in L. Haggarty (ed.), *Teaching Mathematics in Secondary School*. London: RoutledgeFalmer. pp. 33–46.

Noyes, A. (2004a) 'Learning landscapes', *British Educational Research Journal*, 30(1): 27–41.

Noyes, A. (2004b) '(Re)producing mathematics teachers: a sociological perspective', *Teaching Education*, 15(3): 243–56.

Noyes, A. (2006a) 'School transfer and the diffraction of learning trajectories', *Research Papers in Education*, 21(1): 43–62.

Noyes, A. (2006b) 'Using metaphor in mathematics teacher preparation', *Teaching and Teacher Education*, 22(7): 898–909.

Organisation for Economic Co-operation and Development (OECD) (2003) *The PISA 2003 Assessment Framework – Mathematics, Reading, Science and Problem Solving Knowledge and Skills*. Paris: OECD.

Organisation for Economic Co-operation and Development (OECD) (2004) *Learning for Tomorrow's world, First Results from PISA 2003*. Paris: OECD.

Ollerton, M. and A. Watson (2005) *Inclusive Mathematics 11–18*. London: Continuum.

Ortiz-Franco, L. (2005) 'Chicanos have math in their blood', in E. Gutstein and B. Peterson (eds), *Rethinking Mathematics: Teaching Social Justice by the Numbers*. Milwaukee, WI: Rethinking Schools. pp. 70–5.

Paechter, C. (2000) *Changing School Subjects: Power, Gender and Curriculum*. Buckingham: Open University Press.

Pappas, T. (1986) *The Joy of Mathematics – Discovering Mathematics all Around You*. San Carlos, CA: World Wide Publishing.

Popkewitz, T. (2004) 'School subjects, the politics of knowledge, and the projects of intellectuals in change', in P. Valero and R. Zevenbergen (eds), *Researching the Socio-Political Dimensions of Mathematics Education: Issues of Power in Theory and Methodology*. Dordrecht: Kluwer Academic. pp. 251–67.

Povey, H. (2003) 'Teaching and learning mathematics: can the concept of citizenship be reclaimed for social justice?', in L. Burton (ed.), *International Perspectives on Mathematics Education*. Westport, CT: Praeger Publishers: 51–64.

Prestage, S. and P. Perks (2001) *Adapting and Extending Secondary Mathematics Activities: New Tasks for Old*. London: David Fulton.

Qualifications and Curriculum Authority (QCA) (1998) *Education for Citizenship and the Teaching of Democracy in Schools*. London: Qualifications and Curriculum Authority.

Richardson, V. (1996) 'The role of attitudes and beliefs in learning to teach', in J. Sikula, T.J. Buttery and E. Guyton (eds), *Handbook of Research on Teacher Education. A Project of the Association of Teacher Educators*. 2nd edn. London: Prentice Hall International. pp. 102–19.

Rogers, L. (1998) *Society, Mathematics and the Cultural Divide: Ideologies of Policy and Practice 1750–1900*. Mathematics Education and Society 1, Nottingham, England.

Sam, L.C. (2002) 'Public images of mathematics', *Philosophy of Mathematics Education*, 15. Available online @www.people.ex.ac.uk/PErnest/pome15/public_ images.htm (accessed on 12/1/07).

Sautoy, M. du (2003) *The Music of the Primes: Why an Unsolved Problem in Mathematics Matters*. London: Fourth Estate.

Schoenfeld, A. (2002) 'How can we examine the connections between teacher's world views and their educational practices?', *Issues in Education*, 8(2): 217–27.

Scott, D. (2000) *Reading Educational Research and Policy*. London: RoutledgeFalmer.

Sheppard, R. and J. Wilkinson (1994) *Strategy Games*. Diss: Tarquin.

Siefe, C. (2000) *Zero: The Biography of a Dangerous Idea*. London: Souvenir Press.

Singh, S. (2000) *The Code Book*. London: Fourth Estate.

Skovsmose, O. (1994) *Towards a Philosophy of Critical Mathematics Education*. Dordrecht: Kluwer Academic.

Skovsmose, O. (1998) 'Linking mathematics education and democracy: citizenship, mathematical archeology, mathemacy and deliberative action', *Zentralblatt für Didaktik der Mathematik/International Reviews on Mathematics Education*, 30(6): 195–203.

Skovsmose, O. and P. Valero (2002) 'Democratic access to powerful mathematical ideas', in L. English (ed.), *Handbook of International Research in Mathematics Education*. London: Lawrence Erlbaum. pp. 383–407.

Smith, A. (2004) *Making Mathematics Count*. London: The Stationery Office.

Stigler, J. and J. Hiebert (1999). *The Teaching Gap*. New York: Free Press.

The Guardian (2005a) 'Maths was never the most popular ...', 5 July. GuardianUnlimitededucation.guardian.co.uk/egweekly/story/0,,1520968,00.html (accessed 12/1/07 URL).

The Guardian (2005b) 'Hollywood thinks maths is sexy', 24 October. Guardian Unlimitededucation.guardian.co.uk/higher/comment/story/0,,1599479,00.html (accessed 12/1/07 URL).

Tikly, C. and A. Wolf (eds) (2000a) *The Mathematics We Need Now: Demands, Deficits and Remedies*. London: Institute of Education.

Tikly, C. and A. Wolf (2000b) The state of mathematics education', in C. Tikly and A. Wolf (eds), *The Mathematics We Need Now: Demands, Deficits and Remedies*. London: Institute of Education. pp. 1–25.

Thompson, A. (1992) 'Teachers' beliefs and conceptions: a synthesis of research', in D. Grouws (ed.), *Handbook of Research on Mathematics Teaching and Learning*. New York: Macmillan. pp. 209–39.

Volmink, J. (1994) 'Mathematics by all', in S. Lerman (ed.), *Cultural Perspectives on the Mathematics Classroom*. Dordrecht: Kluwer Academic.

Walkerdine, V. (1998) *Counting Girls Out: Girls and Mathematics*. London: Falmer Press.

Watson, A. (1999) 'Working on wonder and wondering: making sense of the spiritual in mathematics teaching', *Mathematics Education Review*, 11: 30–40.

White, J. (2004) *Rethinking the School Curriculum: Values, Aims and Purposes*. London: RoutledgeFalmer.

Wiles, A. (1996) *Horizon: Fermat's Last Theorum*. London BBC. Transcript: www.pbs.org/wgbh/nova/transcripts/2414 proof html accessed 12/1/07.

Winter, J. (2001) 'Personal, spiritual, moral, social and cultural issues in teaching mathematics', in P. Gates (ed.), *Issues in Mathematics Teaching*. London: RoutledgeFalmer.

Winter, R. (1992) '"Mathophobia", Pythogoras and roller-skating', in S. Lerman and M. Nickson (eds), *The Social Context of Mathematics Education: Theory and Practice*. London: South Bank Press. pp. 81–92.

Wolf, A. (2000) 'Mathematics for some or mathematics for all? Curious UK practices in international context', in C. Tikly and A. Wolf (eds), *The Mathematics We Need Now: Demands, Deficits and Remedies*. London: Institute of Education. pp. 104–37.

Wolf, A. (2002) *Does Education Matter?: Myths About Economic Growth*. London: Penguin.

Zevenbergen, R. (2001) 'Language, social class and underachievement in school mathematics', in P. Gates (ed.), *Issues in Mathematics Teaching*. London: RoutledgeFalmer. pp. 38–50.

INDEX